Praise for *H‹*

"Pastor Dane has done us a favor by mining out the gems of the Old Testament where few have gone before. This book should not only be in every pastor's library, but on our coffee tables as well."

— Pastor Gary Galbraith,
Grace Wave Ministries. Author of *Personal Revival*

"Fresh, heartwarming, and insightful. Once I picked it up, I had a difficult time putting it down. Pastor Dane captures these unique and off-the-beaten-path Bible stories with humor and much insight. The Life Lessons section in every chapter are worth the read alone. You will enjoy *Holy Huldah!*"

— Pastor Bill Burnette,
New Life Chapel (Hesperia, California)

"Pastor Dane Davis skillfully lifts stories out of some of the more obscure corners of the Bible. *Holy Huldah!* is a book written both to us and about us—the not-so-famous, very average believers who make up 99 percent of the Kingdom, people who might not think they bring much to the table but by trusting God still somehow manage to change the course of history."

— Pastor Tom Mercer,
High Desert Church,
Author of *8 to 15, The World Is Smaller Than You Think*

Praise for *Holy Huldah!*

"Dane Davis has an eye for the little person, the bit player who steps into the story for a moment, utters a word or two or remains tantalizingly silent, then exits the scene, leaving behind what the author calls 'Life Lessons,' nuggets of wisdom for everyday living."

—Dr. LeRoy Lawson,
Emmanuel Christian Seminary,
Distinguished Professor of Christian Ministries

"Like an investigative journalist, Pastor Davis uncovers the rest of the story and identifies those behind-the-scenes personalities who were influential in some of the high-profile events in the Old Testament. And as an added bonus, Dane provides insightful and practical life applications from each account."

—Dr. John Derry, President,
Hope International University

Holy Huldah!

*Lessons You Should Never
Forget From Bible Characters
You've Never Heard Of*

DANE DAVIS

WESTBOW
PRESS
A DIVISION OF THOMAS NELSON

WestBow Press books may be ordered through booksellers or by contacting:

WestBow Press
A Division of Thomas Nelson
1663 Liberty Drive
Bloomington, IN 47403
www.westbowpress.com
1-(866) 928-1240

All Scripture quotations are from the New International
Version, 1984 edition, unless otherwise specified.

ISBN: 978-1-4497-9826-0 (sc)
ISBN: 978-1-4497-9825-3 (hc)
ISBN: 978-1-4497-9827-7 (e)

Library of Congress Control Number: 2013911501

Printed in the United States of America.

WestBow Press rev. date: 07/24/13

To my church family at First Christian Church of Victorville for praying for me and inspiring me to serve Christ better.

To Holly La Pat, the best administrative assistant and editor on the planet.

To my parents who led me to Christ at a young age.

To my four girls who love me unconditionally and fill my life with laughter.

To my wife Christine, my partner in ministry who loves and supports me at all times. Being a pastor's wife is not easy.

To my Lord and Savior, Jesus Christ. Without Him I'm dust. With Him all things are possible—even writing a book.

TABLE OF CONTENTS

INTRODUCTION

We've all heard of Adam and Eve, David and Goliath, and Daniel in the lion's den. But the question struck me a couple years back: What life lessons could we learn from the hundreds of guys and gals who are mentioned in Scripture that most of us have never heard of, or *have* heard of but ignore? Many books have been written on the life of David. Many commentaries have spotlighted even the smallest details of the lives of Daniel and Jonah. But what about Eliezer of Damascus? What about Shiphrah and Puah? What about Eldad and Medad, Shimei, Micaiah and my all-time favorite, Huldah? Don't these obscure Bible characters deserve our attention as well?

I am convinced that they do. Back in 2010, I spent fourteen weeks leading the congregation I pastor through a study of some of these lesser-known yet enriching Old Testament characters. I discovered that this study has plenty of benefits. For starters, it's a lot of fun and can give us a competitive edge when we play Trivial Pursuit, Bible Edition. But more importantly, this study will impact our lives in three key ways:

#1: The study will help Christians follow God better. Some of these obscure men and women in Scripture demonstrate through their *good* examples how to follow God well. Others teach us through their *bad* examples which pitfalls to avoid. In short, they implore us to be holy like Huldah and avoid being a royal pain in the neck like Shimei.

#2: Studying these ignored Bible characters will offer Christians a unique overview of the Old Testament. Normally when Bible teachers and authors set out to give a summary of the Hebrew Scriptures, they cover the main characters. But could we get a better handle on the big picture of Scripture by shining the spotlight on the minor characters? Absolutely! Over the next ten chapters, we'll cover fourteen hundred years of biblical history in a unique way. We're going to take a tour of Scripture through the eyes of biblical characters that most of us don't know.

#3: The obscurity of these Bible characters will encourage us in our obscurity. The reality is, our lives are obscure. By that I mean that most of us are known by only a few people, and we'll be known by fewer still after we pass. Yet as we examine the lives of these obscure Bible characters, we will see that even though they are known by few and their roles in Scripture are small in comparison to the "big boys" (e.g., Abraham, David and Peter), their lives form an important part of the story of the Bible, God's story. So consider this: If you are a believer and follower of Jesus Christ, God will weave your life into His story regardless of how obscure your life may be to the rest of the world. To say it a different way, your life matters to God because *your* story is an important part of *His* story. Isn't that encouraging?

> Your life matters to God because your story is an important part of His story.

All in all, pulling these nobodies to the foreground and examining their lives has been helpful to the congregation I pastor and to me, and I am convinced that it will be helpful to you as well. And did I mention that it will also be a whole lot of fun? So thank you for taking this journey with me. You won't regret it. Let's discover some lessons we should never forget from these Bible characters we've never heard of. The journey begins.

CHAPTER 1

Eliezer of Damascus

The Guy Who Almost Had It All

For those of you who have a baby on the way or plan to in the not-too-distant future, here is the first of many names that you should be adding to your baby names book: Eliezer of Damascus (pronounced, **"el-ee-EE-zuhr"**). There are already thousands of parents who are naming their baby boys John, Jacob or Michael, so why not be different? Why not swim against the tide? Why not give your handsome baby boy a name that nobody else in the phonebook has—a name like Eliezer of Damascus? Now *that's* a classy name!

Well, you can't say I didn't try.

From Adam to Abram

Our journey through fourteen hundred years of Bible history begins in Genesis 15. Unlike some of the other characters we'll explore in later chapters, Eliezer of Damascus is only mentioned one time in the Bible—in Genesis 15:2. When you read Genesis 15, if your mind wanders for just a second or two, you'll miss him.

Although Genesis 15 is only a few pages into the Bible, over two thousand years of human history had passed by the time

Eliezer stepped onto the scene. The year was about 2000 BC. It had been at least two thousand years since Adam and Eve were kicked out of the garden of Eden and at least three hundred years since the great flood. The LORD had already chosen Abram to be the father of His chosen nation Israel.

God Promises the Impossible

In Genesis 12:2, the LORD said to Abram,

> I will make you into a great nation and I will bless you; I will make your name great, and you will be a blessing. I will bless those who bless you, and whoever curses you I will curse; and all peoples on earth will be blessed through you.

God's promises sounded great, but there was one small problem. Abram and his wife Sarai were too old to have kids. Abram was seventy-five years old, and Sarai was sixty-five. They had been carrying their Middle East AARP cards for several years already. Sarai was well past menopause, but even in her younger years she was unable to have children. Her womb had *always* been barren.

> The LORD wasn't about to let a little thing like impossibility stop Him from fulfilling His promises to Abram.

Now that she was old and gray, Sarai and Abe both knew that she would never give birth to children of her own. Having children at her age was *impossible*! But the LORD wasn't about to let a little thing like impossibility stop Him from fulfilling His promises to Abram. And even though God's promises to Abram were difficult to grasp, Abram tried his best to obey God's commands anyway.

Several years passed, and still no children, not a single one. Abe was getting older. Sarai was getting older. Abram was getting more perplexed when suddenly the LORD broke the silence.

> After this, the word of the LORD came to Abram in a vision: "Do not be afraid, Abram. I am your shield, your very great reward."

> Genesis 15:1

On this occasion, God spoke to Abram in a vision. It's clear from the LORD's words that Abram was startled, even terrified. The LORD said to him, "Do not be afraid, Abram." Sound familiar? When the angel Gabriel appeared to Zechariah, John the Baptist's dad, in the temple, he told him, "Do not be afraid" (Luke 1:13). When Gabriel appeared to Mary and prophesied the birth of Jesus, he told her, "Do not be afraid" (Luke 1:30). When an angel spoke to Joseph, he told him, "Do not be afraid" (Matthew 1:20).

In Scripture, when an angel appears to someone with a message from God, the most common human reaction is absolute terror. And if this was the case when angels appeared to people, how much more true was it when God Himself appeared to people? Here in Genesis 15, the LORD cut through Abram's fear and confusion and told him, "Do not be afraid." As threats against Abram mounted, God reminded him, "I am your shield." And amidst Abram's concerns that the LORD's promises wouldn't pan out, He assured him that He was Abram's "very great reward."

Well, that was all fine and good, but there was still that one *big* problem: It was impossible for Abram's wife Sarai to have kids. The notion that a seventy-five-year-old woman could conceive a child with her eighty-five-year-old husband was preposterous! Can you imagine Sarai saying, "I smell a dirty diaper, Abram. Is it the baby's or is it yours?" And Abram answers back, "I'm not sure. It Depends."

Can you sense Abram's confusion and frustration? He wanted to believe God, but how could he? What God was saying defied all logic. And that's when Abram mentioned good ol' Eliezer of Damascus.

Eliezer: Heir Presumptive?

But Abram said, "O Sovereign LORD, what can you give me since I remain childless and the one who will inherit my estate is Eliezer of Damascus?" And Abram said, "You have given me no children; so a servant in my household will be my heir."

Genesis 15:2-3

Now who on earth is Eliezer of Damascus? According to what Abe says in verse 3, it's clear that Eliezer was one of Abram's household servants. And clearly he was a high-level servant. But that's all that Scripture tells us about him. We have to try to make heads or tails of this notion that Eliezer was to become Abram's heir. Why was Abram convinced that Eliezer would become his heir?

Well, all of the promises the LORD had made to Abram up to this point were contingent upon Abram having a son. In chapter 12, God promised to make Abram into a great nation. That promise could not be fulfilled unless Abram had a son. He certainly wasn't going to be a great nation by himself. God also promised Abram that his name would be great and that all peoples on earth would be blessed through him. Once again, these promises couldn't be fulfilled without a son to be his heir.

In chapter 13:15-16, God promised Abram that his offspring would be like the dust of the earth. They would be innumerable and would inherit all of the land that Abram could see with his eyes. Yet again, these promises were impossible for God to fulfill if Abram remained childless.

So what was Abram to do? Well, evidently he had decided to help God out. In Abram's day and in Abram's culture, if a man didn't have a child (specifically a son) to be his heir after he died, he could adopt one of his slaves to become his heir. Victor Hamilton describes the practice this way in his Genesis commentary:

> All of the promises the LORD had made to Abram up to this point were contingent upon Abram having a son.

> Scholars have noted that Abram's suggestion reflects an adoption procedure…. A childless couple adopts a son, sometimes a slave, to serve them in their lifetime and bury and mourn them when they die. In return for this service they designate the adopted son as the heir presumptive. Should a natural son be born to the couple after such action, this son becomes the chief heir, demoting the adopted son.[1]

Since Abram and Sarai knew it was impossible to have their own biological kids at their ages, it seems that they had already begun to take the legal steps necessary to adopt their servant Eliezer of Damascus. Eliezer would become Abram's heir presumptive

So when the word of the LORD came to Abram here in Genesis 15, Abram was worried about many things, not least of which was the fact that all of God's promises were contingent upon him having an heir. And his only shot at having an heir was to adopt one of his slaves. (No offense, Eliezer, but that's not something that Abe was very excited about.)

But take note of the LORD's response. He didn't scratch His head and say, "Oops, Abe, I forgot all about your wife being barren. I had big plans for you, but you're right—you don't have a true heir to receive My promises. Well, back to the drawing board." No, here's how the LORD actually responded to Abram:

> The word of the LORD came to him: "This man will not be your heir, but a son coming from your own body will be your heir." He took him outside and said, "Look up at the heavens and count the stars—if indeed you can count them." Then he said to him, "So shall your offspring be."
>
> Genesis 15:4-5

Sorry, Eliezer! You are *not* the man. The LORD was determined to make the impossible possible. However, *His* timing would not be *Abram's* timing. Abram would have to wait another fifteen years before the child of the promise would be born. By that time Abram would be one hundred years old and Sarai would be ninety. But through the child of the promise, Isaac, every one of God's promises to Abram would be fulfilled.

> The LORD was determined to make the impossible possible. However, His timing would not be Abram's timing.

And verse 6 records for us one of the most beautiful, life-changing responses to God's word in all of Scripture:

> Abram believed the LORD, and He credited it to him as righteousness.
>
> Genesis 15:6

The New Century Version translates the verse this way:

> Abram believed the LORD. And the LORD accepted Abram's faith, and that faith made him right with God.
>
> Genesis 15:6

Surprisingly, here in chapter 15 God didn't give Abram a shred of evidence that His promises would be fulfilled. He *illustrated* His promise by pointing him to the stars, but He didn't offer him any evidence. God didn't give Abram a picture of what Isaac would look like. He didn't give him a sneak peak of a home movie that would be taken in twenty years. The only evidence that God offered Abram was His own word itself.

And when Abram received God's word, he believed it to be true just as if the LORD had given him all the evidence in the world. Abram believed the word of the LORD, and as a result, God credited it to him as righteousness. The writer of Hebrews reminds us of the great importance of believing in God and His word:

Without faith [belief] it is impossible to please God, because anyone who comes to Him must believe that He exists and that He rewards those who earnestly seek Him.

Hebrews 11:6

Friends, one of the most righteous things you can do is to *believe* and *trust* the word of the LORD. Sometimes God's word doesn't make *sense* to our five senses, but if you have chosen to follow Jesus Christ as Lord and Savior, you have chosen to walk by *faith*, not by sight. We must learn to *trust* God's word more than we trust our own five senses. We must learn to *believe* God's word more than we believe our own experiences, our own feelings and our own instincts. We must learn to believe the word of the LORD.

Abram did. And fifteen years later, at the tender age of one hundred, he held a healthy baby boy in his arms. I wonder if Eliezer himself held little Isaac in his arms, shaking his head in amazement.

3 Life Lessons

Life Lesson #1: A Lesson from God: God is not limited by our impossibilities. Is it impossible for a ninety-year-old woman to have a baby? Absolutely! But I want you to answer a simple question for me: "Who's bigger: God or impossible?" You know the answer: God is bigger! Are certain things impossible? Sure, but God is bigger than impossible.

Mary had to come to grips with this reality when the angel Gabriel came to her and told her that she was going to have a son. Is it impossible for a virgin to have a child? Sure it is! They didn't have artificial insemination or in vitro fertilization in Bible times. So it was impossible. But did that stop God? Nope. He made the impossible possible. God is not limited by our impossibilities.

So take heart if you find yourself in an impossible situation today. Perhaps you believe it is impossible for you to pay your bills with the money you have available, or you think it's impossible to ever have

> Who's bigger:
> God or impossible?

a happy marriage because you and your spouse have hurt each other so badly. Possibly you're convinced that it's impossible for your medical condition to ever improve. After all, even the doctors have offered you no hope for recovery.

Take heart! God whispers to you today the same words that He spoke to Abram some 4,000 years ago: "Look up at the heavens and count the stars—if indeed you can count them." Friend, your Creator did the impossible when He formed this universe and hung every star in the sky. So He can do the impossible again in *your* life. A problem that for you is impossible to fix is a piece of cake for God. So turn to the LORD. He specializes in the impossible.

Life Lesson #2: A Lesson from Abe: One of the most God-pleasing things you can ever do is to actively believe the word

of the LORD. Notice how I used the word "actively." I include the word "actively" because all you have to do is scan down a few verses in Genesis 15 to see that Abe obeyed *every* instruction the LORD gave him as the LORD made a covenant with Abram. That's the litmus test of true faith in God. If you really *believe* the word of the LORD, you will *act* upon it. You will *obey* the word of the LORD and *walk in step* with the word of the LORD. There are plenty of people in our lives who claim to *believe* in God, but their lives reveal the truth: They aren't *followers* of God.

> That's the litmus test of true faith in God. If you really believe the word of the LORD, you will act upon it and obey it.

The Greek word for faith is *pisteuo*, and it's a very interesting word. Although it is oftentimes translated as "belief" in the New Testament, it means much more than intellectual belief. Biblical faith involves mind, body and spirit. It is active. It is lived out. It is animated. For that reason I like to use the synonym "trust" in place of belief. To our English-speaking brains the word *trust* better communicates that our belief and faith in God must be active.

If it is not active, as James points out in James 2:17, it is *dead* faith. So don't allow your faith to become dead. Actively believe the word of the LORD. Actively believe that He will supply all of your needs according to His glorious riches in Christ Jesus (Philippians 4:19).

Life Lesson #3: A Lesson from Eliezer of Damascus: Sometimes it looks like you're about to get a big break, but your hopes and dreams get shattered. When that happens, stay faithful where God has placed you, and trust Him. We never read of Eliezer of Damascus again in Scripture, and I think that's a very good thing. We don't read of Eliezer throwing a "pity party" after Abram's son was born. No indication is given that Eliezer took out his aggression on Isaac. We don't read of even a single complaint or whimper from Eliezer. Evidently, he stayed faithful to his master Abram in obscurity.

Like you and me, Eliezer will never be remembered alongside the great heroes of Scripture. His name will never be written on banners or honored by Sunday school children. But that's okay. It was all part of the LORD's plan, and I believe with all my heart that His plan is always best.

Like Eliezer, you and I don't need our names posted on Sunday school flannel boards or published in Bible study curriculum books. We don't need to have our names placed alongside the great biblical heroes of our faith: Abraham, David, Joshua, Noah, Esther, Ruth, Daniel and Paul. We don't even need to have our names placed alongside the names of modern-day Christian heroes like Billy Graham or James Dobson.

If God chooses to make us well-known, that's fine and good. That's His choice. But that should never be *our* goal. After all, God has not called us to be *famous*. He has called us to be *faithful*. I encourage you to trust Him and faithfully serve Him in the midst of your obscurity, just like Eliezer of Damascus.

CHAPTER 2

Shiphrah & Puah

The Two Ladies Who Foiled Pharaoh's Plan

Have you ever heard of a man named Otto Beckenhauer? How about Robert Porter Burns? No? Well, these names may mean nothing to you, but they mean a lot to me. Each of these men impacted my life in important ways as I was growing up. Their lives helped shape my life. In His grace God used both their words and examples to help shape my character and point me to Christ.

You see, Otto Beckenhauer was my fourth grade Sunday school teacher: a somewhat grouchy old fellow who challenged me to memorize key parts of the Bible. Under his tutelage I learned all sixty-six books of the Bible, the Beatitudes (Matthew 5:1-12) and the LORD's Prayer. And Mr. Beckenhauer used a teaching technique that every fourth grade Sunday school teacher should master: *bribery*. I don't remember the details of the smaller awards handed out throughout the year, but I remember the crème de la crème—the grand prize awarded to me at the end of the school year—a brand new Bible. I will never forget this gray-haired teacher with the funny name who motivated me to memorize key parts of God's word.

Robert Porter Burns was my grandfather. I called him "Poppy," and although he died before my ninth birthday, he modeled for me how a *strong* man can have a *soft* heart. He was a faithful and loving husband. Whenever my sister and I talked my grandmother into doing a back flip off the swimming pool diving board—yes, my sixty-eight-year-old grandma could do back flips—Poppy was always treading water in the deep end, reassuring her that he was right there to catch her. And he was equally nurturing to my sister and me. Even when I (in my childish enthusiasm) jumped into his bed early in the morning and handed him my toy bear to play with, he smiled, laughed and cheerfully played along. He made it clear to me that I was more important to him than a few more minutes of sleep. I hope that one day I can be as loving and tender a "poppy" to my grandkids as he was to me.

> Poppy made it clear to me that I was more important to him than a few more minutes of sleep.

I would guess that you, like me, can recall some people who nobody else may remember but *you* will never forget. These individuals made a profound impact on your life. Maybe it was a teacher or a neighbor, an uncle or a coach. Maybe it was even a doctor or good Samaritan who saved your life. Their names may escape you, but their deeds never will. Whoever these unsung heroes are, they helped shape your young life and mold you into the man or woman that you are today. If your life tells a story, their lives helped write several chapters of it. Don't you thank God for them?

In Exodus chapter 1, we will discover two of the unsung heroes of the Bible whose obscure lives helped set the nation of Israel on course. These two women had funny names, but their heroics were nothing to laugh at. Their bold stance for the LORD and His people resulted in hundreds, maybe even thousands of young lives being saved. These ladies' names were Shiphrah (pronounced, "**SHIF-ruh**") and Puah (pronounced, "**PYOO-uh**").

From Abram to Moses

It had been about five hundred years since God spoke to Abram in Genesis 15. The LORD had promised to make Abram into a great nation, and that's exactly what He did. Fifteen years after the LORD told Abram that Eliezer wouldn't become his heir, God blessed Abram and Sarai with a son of their own. His name was Isaac, and he was surprisingly healthy for a baby boy born to a ninety-year-old mom and a one hundred-year-old dad.

As the years passed, Isaac had two sons of his own: Jacob and Esau. God changed Jacob's name to Israel, and his descendants became the twelve tribes of Israel. Through a bizarre set of circumstances, the LORD paved the way for Jacob's son Joseph to become the second most powerful leader in Egypt. God gave Joseph the ability to accurately prophesy the coming of a devastating seven-year famine. The LORD also gave him the insight and management skills necessary to assemble the world's largest supply of emergency rations in preparation for the great famine. His actions saved thousands of Egyptians' lives as well as the lives of his own family.

At the end of Genesis, Israel and his seventy-member family migrated to Egypt, and it was there in Egypt that one of the LORD's greatest promises to Abram was fulfilled. In the

> It was in Egypt that one of the LORD's greatest promises to Abram was fulfilled.

time span of four hundred years, the population of Israel swelled from seventy to several hundred thousand. Israel was on the verge of becoming a "great nation" indeed, but not everyone was ready to stand up and celebrate.

The Stage Is Set For a Showdown

Now Joseph and all his brothers and all that generation died, but the Israelites were fruitful and multiplied greatly and became exceedingly numerous, so that the land was filled with them. Then a new king, who did not know about Joseph, came to power in Egypt.

Exodus 1:6-8

Here in these verses Moses (the author of Exodus) highlights three very important realities that set the stage for a great showdown between the God of Israel and the Pharaoh of Egypt.

The first reality was that Joseph's entire generation was long gone. The Israelites here in Exodus 1 were at least ten generations removed from the original seventy who migrated to Egypt. Around three hundred years had passed.

The second reality was that while they were in Egypt, the Israelites experienced a population explosion. When Moses uses the word "multiplied greatly and became exceedingly numerous" he means just that. Eighty years later when Moses would lead the Israelites out of captivity in Egypt, we read in Exodus 12:37 that there were about 600,000 men besides women and children. So here in Exodus chapter 1, we're likely looking at a total population of over half a million.

That kind of population growth isn't too shabby, don't you think? Three hundred years earlier when Israel was a tiny nation of only seventy people, the Egyptians thought they were harmless enough. But here in Exodus 1, Israel was no longer a measly little nation. Israel was a massive group of people living in Egypt's backyard, and the Egyptians began to resent and fear them.

The third reality was that a new Pharaoh rose to power in Egypt, and he didn't know about Joseph. Now, if the chapter stopped right here, we could probably guess what was going to happen next. All three of these realities made for a tense situation: #1) Joseph's generation was long gone. The one who saved the day in the time of the great famine was ancient history. #2) The Israelite nation had grown like wildfire. #3) A new Pharaoh arose who didn't know about the Israelites' superhero ancestor. Even if he *had* known about Joseph, he probably wouldn't have cared.

There's an old saying: *No good deed goes unpunished.* Joseph's good deed in saving Egypt brought him and his family much appreciation and respect during his lifetime. But it didn't take long for his good deed to be completely ignored and even resented.

Verses 9-10 allow us to eavesdrop on Pharaoh's conversation with his high level advisors:

> "Look," he said to his people, "the Israelites have become much too numerous for us. Come, we must deal shrewdly with them or they will become even more numerous and, if war breaks out, will join our enemies, fight against us and leave the country."
>
> Exodus 1:9-10

This new Pharaoh who "did not know about Joseph" was not interested in the good that the Israelites *had done* in generations past. He was only interested in the harm they *could do* in generations future. His reaction here in verses 9-10 was a reaction of fear. And we all know that fear is a powerful motivator.

> This new Pharaoh was not interested in the good that the Israelites *had* done. He was only interested in the harm they *could* do.

Pharaoh feared the *culture* of Israel. They lived and worshiped so differently from the way the Egyptians did. Pharaoh feared the *allegiance* of Israel. He wasn't convinced that they were devoted to his country. But most of all he feared the *size* of Israel. He knew that if they revolted or joined forces with one of Egypt's enemies, Egypt would be in deep, deep trouble.

3 Tactics – 3 Failures

So fear drove Pharaoh to be a ruthless tyrant, and he used three different tactics in an attempt to keep the Israelite nation from growing any larger or staging a revolt. Pharaoh's first tactic is revealed in verses 11-14.

> So they put slave masters over them to oppress them with forced labor, and they built Pithon and Rameses as store cities for Pharaoh. But the more they were oppressed, the more they multiplied and spread; so the Egyptians came to dread the Israelites and worked them ruthlessly. They made their lives bitter with hard labor in brick and mortar and with all kinds of work in the fields; in all their hard labor the Egyptians used them ruthlessly.
>
> Exodus 1:11-14

Pharaoh's first tactic was to oppress the Israelites with slavery. Pharaoh instructed the Egyptian slave masters to work the Israelites to the bone. Pharaoh was convinced that hard, bitter labor would thin out the Israelite ranks. Surely, many of the men would buckle under the pressure and die of stress and heat exhaustion while many of the younger women would miscarry as a result of fatigue and injury. But as verse 12 points out so clearly, "The more they were oppressed, the more they multiplied and spread."

A ruthless tyrant and his band of slave-driving cronies weren't going to keep God from carrying out His promise to Abram. Israel was going to continue to grow into a great nation despite Pharaoh's ruthlessness.

All of Egypt's human wisdom and experience had led Pharaoh to believe that if he worked the Israelites ruthlessly, their population would shrink. There would be *no way* that the Israelite population could continue growing under these conditions. But Pharaoh had never before dealt with the hand of God. He didn't understand that God's blessing will always trump man's curse.

> **Pharaoh didn't understand that God's blessing will always trump man's curse.**

The LORD had made a covenant promise to Abraham that He was going to make his descendents into a great nation. And nothing was going to stop Him from keeping His covenant promise: not a slave master, not Pharaoh, *nobody*.

As a result, Pharaoh's first tactic failed miserably. No matter how harsh the slave masters were to the Israelites, their population kept growing. So Pharaoh tried a second tactic in verses 15-21, and this is where Shiphrah and Puah came onto the scene:

> The king of Egypt said to the Hebrew midwives, whose names were Shiphrah and Puah, "When you help the Hebrew women in childbirth and observe them on the delivery stool, if it is a boy, kill him; but if it is a girl, let her live."
>
> Exodus 1:15-16

Pharaoh's second tactic was to order the Hebrew midwives (Shiphrah and Puah) to murder all the Hebrew baby boys. Here in Exodus 1:15 is the only time in the Bible that Shiphrah and Puah are mentioned by name. As God's story unfolds in the pages of the Bible, these two Jewish ladies had their stories woven into God's story. And the question is: Did they stand on Pharaoh's side or on God's side? Would they forever be known as heroes or villains? The choice was theirs.

Let's take a few moments to get acquainted with these two ladies. Who were Shiphrah and Puah? Well, all that we know about these ladies is found here in Exodus 1. We are told that they were "the Hebrew midwives," and Moses emphasizes that their job was to "help the Hebrew women in childbirth." Now, with several hundred thousand Israelites living in Egypt, it's safe to assume that these two women couldn't possibly be present at every Hebrew birth. That being the case, they were most likely the *head* midwives. You can think of them as the CEOs of Hebrew Midwives, Inc., possibly overseeing several dozen midwives who assisted with Israelite births.

Since there weren't any obstetricians to deliver babies, families relied upon these midwives to ensure safe deliveries. And it was Shiphrah and Puah's job to ensure proper training and quality control. They established the policies and procedures and disseminated them throughout the ranks of midwives. So when Pharaoh decided to have all of the Hebrew baby boys murdered at birth, he gave his order directly to Shiphrah and Puah. As the supervisors of the Hebrew midwives, it would be Shiphrah and Puah's job to ensure that every midwife followed Pharaoh's orders to kill every baby boy.

Pharaoh's instructions were crystal clear, but notice Shiphrah and Puah's courageous response:

> The midwives, however, feared God and did not do what the king of Egypt had told them to do; they let the boys live.
>
> Exodus 1:17

What a great verse! Pharaoh had the power to snap his fingers and have these women thrown in jail, tortured or put to death. But these women feared God more than they feared Pharaoh. In Luke 12:4-5 Jesus taught his disciples who they should and shouldn't fear:

"I tell you, my friends, do not be afraid of those who kill the body and after that can do no more. But I will show you whom you should fear: Fear Him who, after the killing of the body, has power to throw you into hell."

Luke 12:4-5

Friends, no person on earth can touch your soul or spirit. This being the case, no man on earth can touch your eternal life. So we don't have to fear *man*. But it is good and proper to fear *God*. If we don't fear God enough to respect and obey His laws, then we are cruisin' for an eternal bruisin'. Pharaoh's word was, "Kill the baby boys." God's word was "Thou shalt not kill." Shiphrah and Puah wisely chose to obey God rather than man even if it cost them their lives.

In verse 18 the inevitable happened: Pharaoh discovered that Shiphrah and Puah had disobeyed his direct order, and he was furious:

> Shiphrah and Puah "feared God and did not do what the king of Egypt had told them to do; they let the boys live." (Exodus 1:17)

Then the king of Egypt summoned the midwives and asked them, "Why have you done this? Why have you let the boys live?"

Exodus 1:18

Uh oh! It was one thing for Shiphrah and Puah to ignore the king's command when he wasn't looking, but now they were being forced to defend their actions to his face.

I can just imagine several of Pharaoh's bodyguards standing on both sides of Shiphrah and Puah. With one word from the king, the lives of these women could be terminated in a matter of seconds. Shiphrah and Puah had just one chance to defend their actions, and if they valued their lives, they had better speak shrewdly. This would be the perfect opportunity for Shiphrah and Puah to heed the advice that Jesus would give 1,500 years later: "Be as shrewd as snakes and as innocent as doves" (Matthew 10:16).

Well, listen to Shiphrah and Puah's shrewd response to Pharaoh in verse 19:

> The midwives answered Pharaoh, "Hebrew women are not like Egyptian women; they are vigorous and give birth before the midwives arrive."
>
> Exodus 1:19

Now, to be honest with you, I'm not sure if these ladies were telling the truth or flat out lying. But my hunch is that Shiphrah and Puah had developed a shrewd way to ensure safe deliveries without physically being in the delivery room for the entire process. Maybe they delivered each baby's head and shoulders and then quickly left the room, allowing a family member to finish the delivery so they wouldn't be on scene when the gender of the baby was revealed. Or perhaps they began teaching family members how to deliver babies safely so that the midwives wouldn't have to be in the room for *any* part of the delivery. Regardless of the specifics of *how* they avoided having to carry out Pharaoh's command, of two things there is no doubt: Shiphrah and Puah feared God far more than Pharaoh, and they were very shrewd in their dealings with Pharaoh. As a result, God blessed them.

> So God was kind to the midwives and the people increased and became even more numerous. And because the midwives feared God, He gave them families of their own.
>
> Exodus 1:20-21

When it came to Pharaoh's efforts to curb the growth of the Israelite nation, he was 0-for-2 with his first two tactics. He oppressed the Israelites with bitter slavery, but their population continued to grow. Then he ordered the Hebrew midwives to kill all newborn baby boys, but that didn't work either. So Pharaoh tried a third and final tactic:

> Then Pharaoh gave this order to all his people: "Every boy that is born you must throw into the Nile, but let every girl live."
>
> Exodus 1:22

Pharaoh's third tactic to curb the Israelite population was to have his soldiers drown every Hebrew baby boy in the Nile River. But as we quickly discover in chapter 2, that didn't work either. In fact, the river that Pharaoh intended to bring death to the Israelites, the LORD used to bring life.

A little Hebrew boy named Moses was placed in the Nile River and eighty years later was used by God to deliver the Israelites out of slavery in Egypt once and for all. Moses' helpless cries as a young infant floating in a reed basket would one day become the cries of a great deliverer who would confront Pharaoh and demand, "Let my people go!"

> Moses' helpless cries as a young infant floating down the Nile would one day become the cries of a great deliverer who would confront Pharaoh and demand, "Let my people go!"

3 Life Lessons

Life Lesson #1: A Lesson from God: The LORD will fulfill His covenant promises no matter what men do to try to stop Him.

Common sense tells us that every one of Pharaoh's tactics *should* have worked. Overworking the Israelites as slaves *should* have reduced their population. Ordering the midwives to murder all baby boys *should* have curbed the nation's growth. And tossing the Hebrew baby boys into the Nile River *should* have driven the final nail in their population-growth coffin. But it didn't.

Why not? How could each and every one of these sure-fire tactics have failed? The answer is simple and straightforward: No slave master, no Pharaoh, no crocodile in the Nile can stop God from carrying out His promise of blessing to His chosen people. As we are reminded by the Apostle Paul: **"If God is for us, who can be against us?"** (Romans 8:31).

> No slave master, no Pharaoh, no crocodile in the Nile can stop God from carrying out His promise of blessing to His chosen people.

Friend, when you are under attack, be encouraged. If God has promised to bless you, He *will* bless you. Nothing man can do to you will stop God from fulfilling His promises of blessing.

Life Lesson #2: A Lesson from Pharaoh: If you are fighting against God, you are fighting a losing battle. It doesn't matter how smart you are; it doesn't matter how strong you are; it doesn't matter how confident you are; it doesn't matter how good-looking you are. If you fight against the LORD and His plan and His purposes, you *will* lose. Period. Friends, it makes much more sense to get on board with God's plan and obey God's rules, because if we don't, we *will* be on the losing side of the battle both in this life and in eternity. So if you find yourself fighting against God, stop it! It's a fight you can not win. Don't be a fool like Pharaoh. Fight *for* God, not against Him.

Life Lesson #3: A Lesson from Shiphrah and Puah: When we fear and obey God, He will pour out His kindness and blessing on us. Human wisdom screamed out to the midwives: "If you disobey Pharaoh, he will have your heads!" But throughout the pages of the Bible, the reality rings clearly: God's blessing *always* trumps man's cursing. Pharaoh might have been piping mad, but Shiphrah and Puah were safe under the covering of God's covenant blessing. So don't worry yourself with man's threats and curses as long as you are living in obedience to the LORD. *He* is the One you should want to please. *His* favor is the favor you should seek. And if you are living underneath the shelter of His blessings, none of your enemies' curses can touch you.

Like Eliezer of Damascus, Shiphrah and Puah are "nobodies" in Scripture. Their names will probably never be hung on banners. They won't be praised and honored by Sunday school children. But because they feared the LORD and obeyed His commands, their God-honoring actions will forever be woven into the pages of God's story. You and I may forget their names within the next twenty minutes, but God will *never* forget their names or what they did for Him and His chosen people. And their reward in Heaven will last forever. Can the same be said of you?

CHAPTER 3

Eldad & Medad

The Two Prophets Who Skipped Church

During my sophomore year in college, some friends and I did something during our spring break that I'll never forget: We built a house. The college I attended had a close relationship with Amor Ministries, a wonderful organization that specializes in assembling short-term volunteer teams to build homes for impoverished families in Mexico. The two-room houses Amor missions teams build look more like large sheds by American standards, but they can be built quickly and cheaply, and they are significantly nicer than poor families' existing homes.

On this occasion our team built a home for a family of five who lived in a small garage-door house. In the aftermath of the devastating Tijuana floods of the early 1990s, thousands of used garage doors were delivered to the outskirts of Tijuana that could be used to assemble a temporary structure. Four garage doors provided four walls, and two more could make a roof. And for the family whose new home we were building, rolled-up clothes and towels provided wind blocks between the walls and the roof. As you might guess, there was no indoor plumbing or hard-wired electricity. It was a sobering scene to behold. To say that these living conditions were modest would be a gross understatement.

Yet despite these primitive living conditions, when I think back on the three days I spent on the outskirts of Tijuana, there is one specific image that stands out in my memory: the image of the family's three children playing on a pile of dirt beside the house, smiling as if they were the happiest children on earth. By American standards, those kids had "nothing." But their faces radiated a joy that I rarely see on the faces of American children who have by comparison, "everything": large homes, indoor plumbing, iPods, cable or satellite TV, video game systems, and the list goes on and on.

I know that our little missions team was a blessing to that Mexican family, but they didn't realize how much of a blessing they were to me. They taught me much about contentment and joy. And, unknowingly, they reminded me of this truth: Some of the greatest work that Christians can ever do is *outside* the church building. Therefore, if we as Christians restrict our

> Some of the greatest work that Christians can ever do is outside the church building.

work to what can be done on church property, our impact in this world will always be limited. God has never restricted His movement to the confines of the church building, and neither should we. If you don't believe me, just ask Eldad (pronounced, "**EL-dad**") and Medad (pronounced, "**ME-dad**").

A Pivotal 40-Year Period

Eighty years after baby Moses floated down the Nile River in a reed basket, he stood before Pharoah and delivered the LORD's command: "Let My people go!" Ten plagues later, that's exactly what Pharoah did. He let God's people, Israel, leave Egypt. And off they went to claim the Promised Land that God had promised some six hundred years earlier to Abraham.

The book of Exodus (from chapter 13 on), along with the books of Leviticus, Numbers and Deuteronomy, highlight forty crucial years of Jewish history. There are a number of reasons why God dedicates so much time in Scripture to these forty years, but I'll highlight just three.

#1: They provide a detailed historical record of one of the most significant events in Jewish history: the forty-year journey from Egypt to the Promised Land of Canaan, which would eventually become the homeland of Israel.

#2: These four books record God's 613 laws that the nation of Israel was required to follow. Together the first five books of the Bible are called by several names including The Books of Moses, the Pentateuch and the Torah. They spell out in great detail what the God of Israel required of His people as the terms of their covenant with Him.

#3: These four books provide a case study on how God deals with grumbling and complaining.

Now, this third reason should probably *not* be placed on the same level of importance as the first two, but nonetheless, it is important. And our new friends, Eldad and Medad, will help us understand just *how* important. Numbers 11 provides one of the greatest examples of how both God and Moses dealt with the Israelites' complaining.

The Riff-Raff Complain

By the time we reach Numbers chapter 11, it had been just over a year since the Israelites were delivered from slavery in Egypt. By this point, Israel had already crossed the Red Sea, witnessed the decimation of Pharoah's army and received the Ten

Commandments. Once again the Israelites pulled up stakes and edged closer to the Promised Land.

And as they went they started doing something that they were very good at: *complaining*. During this period, the Israelites were perpetual pessimists and glorious gripers. The food was too bland. The water was too scarce. The glass was always half-empty. The Israelites *could* complain and *did* complain about anything and everything. This was certainly the case here in Numbers 11. And it was in the midst of God addressing this complaining that we're introduced to two unknown guys: Eldad and Medad.

> The rabble with them began to crave other food, and again the Israelites started wailing and said, "If only we had meat to eat! We remember the fish we ate in Egypt at no cost—also the cucumbers, melons, leeks, onions and garlic. But now we have lost our appetite; we never see anything but this manna!"
>
> Numbers 11:4-6

Verse 4 refers to some of the people as "rabble." *The Message* translation uses the word "riff-raff." The riff-raff among the Israelites began to complain about the manna as they had flashbacks to the buffets in Egypt. Back in the land of slavery they had enjoyed all sorts of fresh fish and vegetables, but here in the wilderness they just had one food item: manna. Manna for breakfast. Manna for lunch. Manna for dinner. Manna, manna, manna!

The riff-raff started grumbling and complaining, and grumbling and complaining usually leads to what? *More* grumbling and complaining. Grumbling and complaining can be very contagious, and it certainly was among the Israelites. The grumbling spread like wildfire through the Israelite camp as did a chronic case of selective memory syndrome. As they reminisced about their former lives in Egypt, they remembered the fish, the watermelon, the leeks, the onions and the garlic. But they seemed to have forgotten the slavery: the ruthless workload, the beatings and the drowned babies.

Within the next few verses we discover that this round of complaining really took its toll on Moses. This was not the first time that the Israelites had complained since leaving Egypt. It wasn't even the second, third or fourth time. They had complained about the pursuing army of Pharoah. They had complained about being thirsty. They had complained about being hungry. They had complained about Moses being gone for too long on Mt. Sinai, and when he finally *did* come down the mountain, they complained about his face shining too brightly with God's radiance.

> They remembered the fish, the watermelon, the leeks, the onions and the garlic. But they seemed to have forgotten the slavery: the ruthless workload, the beatings and the drowned babies.

These people were a bunch of whining crybabies, and Moses was fed up with them. He basically cried out, "Enough, LORD! Enough! I can't take it any more! I can't stand to hear another single complaint! These people look like adults, but they whine like a bunch of two-year-olds!"

The LORD Meets Moses' Need

Moses had reached his breaking point, so the LORD chose to act. He met Moses' need in two very significant ways. First, He addressed the burden of Moses' workload. Listen to God's words to Moses in verses 16 and 17:

> The LORD said to Moses: "Bring me seventy of Israel's elders who are known to you as leaders and officials among the people. Have them come to the Tent of Meeting, that they may stand there with you. I will come down and

speak with you there, and I will take of the Spirit that is on you and put the Spirit on them. They will help you carry the burden of the people so that you will not have to carry it alone."

Numbers 11:16-17

The first way that the LORD met Moses' need was to provide seventy associate pastors to help shoulder the burden of leadership. The second way He addressed Moses' need was by giving the complaining people exactly what they asked for: meat...lots and lots of it. God gave Moses these instructions:

Tell the people: "Consecrate yourselves in preparation for tomorrow, when you will eat meat. The LORD heard you when you wailed, 'If only we had meat to eat! We were better off in Egypt!' Now the LORD will give you meat, and you will eat it. You will not eat it for just one day, or two days, or five, ten or twenty days. But for a whole month—until it comes out of your nostrils and you loathe it—because you have rejected the LORD, who is among you, and have wailed before him saying, 'Why did we ever leave Egypt?'"

Numbers 11:18-20

Can you imagine what was going through Moses' mind as God promised to meet his needs? My guess is that Moses was silently celebrating: "Thank You, LORD! Thank You! Thank You! Thank You!" Not only was God responding to the Israelites' complaints by giving them more meat than they could possibly eat, God was also providing seventy associate pastors for Moses to help shoulder the burden and stress of dealing with the Israelites' future complaining.

Here Come Eldad and Medad

Now just a few verses further down, we're introduced to two of the seventy elders Moses chose to help shoulder his leadership burden. Their names were—you guessed it—Eldad and Medad. The reason they are mentioned is because they missed out on what may have been the most important meeting of their lives. Just as the LORD had instructed, Moses summoned the seventy hand-picked elders to meet him at the Tent of Meeting (aka, the tabernacle).

God's plan seemed foolproof. With the seventy elders gathered around Moses at the tabernacle, God's Spirit would descend and speak to Moses. Then the LORD would take some of His presence (Spirit) from Moses and apportion it to the seventy elders gathered with him. It was a great plan. Easy smeezy! Slam dunk! Right? Well, not so fast...

There was a small problem. Seventy elders were summoned to the tabernacle, but only sixty-eight showed up. Eldad and Medad had gone AWOL. They had evidently received the memo about the meeting, but for some reason they didn't show up. But that didn't stop the LORD from proceeding with His plan.

The rest of the seventy elders gathered at the Tent of Meeting with Moses. The LORD came down in a cloud and spoke with him, and then He took of the Spirit that was on Moses and put it on the sixty-eight. And according to verse 25, when God did this the elders began to prophesy. What their prophecies were and how long they were spoken, we're not told. But

> Eldad and Medad had gone AWOL. They had evidently received the memo, but for some reason they didn't show up.

clearly these sixty-eight elders were speaking fresh, intelligible truths from God that could not have been spoken unless He had revealed them.

So did Eldad and Medad miss out on the prophesying since they were absent from the meeting? Interestingly…no. According to verse 26, Eldad and Medad remained in the camp, but as the Spirit of God descended upon the other sixty-eight elders at the Tent of Meeting, His Spirit *also* descended upon them. So like the others, Eldad and Medad began prophesying right on the spot where the Spirit had found them—right there in the camp. Revelations of God's truth poured forth from their mouths that were clear evidence of the anointing of God's Spirit. Well, word about Eldad and Medad's prophesying spread quickly.

> A young man ran and told Moses, "Eldad and Medad are prophesying in the camp."
>
> Numbers 11:27

While Eldad and Medad's prophesying may seem like a good thing to you and me, some in Moses' leadership circle didn't agree, including Joshua.

> Joshua son of Nun, who had been Moses' aide since youth, spoke up and said, "Moses, my lord, stop them."
>
> Numbers 11:28

Joshua was confident that Eldad and Medad had received Moses' memo. He knew that they had been given explicit instructions to join Moses at the tabernacle. So it seems that he believed that they, as no-shows, had forfeited their right to receive the commission of leadership, and, along with it, their right to prophesy. After all, Moses' top leaders couldn't just start wandering through the camp speaking God's word all willy-nilly. That would be disrespectful to Moses. Wouldn't it? And that could hurt Moses' feelings. Couldn't it? But Moses set Joshua straight:

> "Are you jealous for my sake? I wish that all the LORD's people were prophets and that the LORD would put His Spirit on them!"
>
> Numbers 11:29

As one who had just poured out his complaint to the LORD, Moses had a much different perspective on Eldad and Medad's prophesying than did Joshua. Moses was tired of feeling like he was the only person in all Israel who heard God speak and was able, in turn, to speak to the people for God. He was elated that the LORD's Spirit would now be speaking *to* and *through* seventy other men, and he wasn't going to sweat the details. Sure, Eldad and Medad had been instructed to come to the tabernacle, but if God was willing to overlook their absence (as indicated by anointing them with His Spirit), who was Moses to question Him or reject the elders whom He had blessed? After all, Moses' leadership was never about honoring and glorifying *himself* but instead about honoring and glorifying *the LORD*. According to the Book of Numbers:

> Moses was a very humble man, more humble than anyone else on the face of the earth.
>
> Numbers 12:3

As a pastor I can't help but wonder how much easier ministry would be if God's Spirit rested heavily on every single Christian in the Church. If we had more of the Spirit of Jesus inside us, I'm confident that we would *complain* less and *pray* more. If we had more of the Spirit inside of us, we would *share* our leaders' burdens instead of *adding* to their burdens.

3 Life Lessons

Lesson #1: A Lesson from the Riff-Raff: When God has met your needs, don't complain about how He did so. God is perfect, and the way He provides for you is always perfect. To criticize His blessings is to criticize His character. If we are honest with ourselves, we have to admit that we, like the Israelites, can be very greedy and unappreciative. We have a bad habit of *grumbling* about our jobs instead of *thanking God* that we have a job, *criticizing* our spouses and kids' faults instead of *praising* them for their strengths, and *cursing* our leaders with our complaints instead of *blessing* them with our prayers.

Friend, there may be times when your food is cold and your boss is even colder. But God loves you, and He is your perfect Provider. So please…rise above the riff-raff. Stop treating God's blessings as if they were curses. He is good to you, so thank Him for His goodness.

> Rise above the riff-raff. Stop treating God's blessings as if they were curses. He is good to you, so thank Him for His goodness.

> Give thanks in all circumstances, for this is God's will for you in Christ Jesus.
>
> 1 Thessalonians 5:18

Lesson #2: A Lesson from Moses: Even the greatest leaders need others around them to shoulder the burdens of leadership. When the burdens of leadership are too heavy, lean on God

and lean on others. I am so thankful for the example of Moses. Moses was a phenomenal leader! For forty years he served the LORD faithfully and led some two million Israelites from slavery in Egypt to the front door of the Promised Land. He was a consistent, humble role model. He was a fervent pray-er. He was a disciplined law keeper. He had an unearthly amount of patience with gripers and complainers. And he loved his people fiercely. On more than one occasion when God threatened to destroy the Israelites because of their sins, Moses dropped to his knees and lovingly interceded to the LORD on their behalf.

Yet here in Numbers 11, we see that *even Moses* couldn't shoulder the burdens of leadership alone. As hard as Moses tried, he couldn't escape this reality: No *one* man could consistently and effectively lead this huge nation of people. It just couldn't be done. He needed help. So the LORD lovingly raised up assistant leaders for Moses: Eldad, Medad and sixty-eight of their fellow elders.

If you have been called to carry out a great leadership task for the LORD and you are doing it all alone…stop it! Ask God to provide helpers to support you in His work, and when He sends them, don't chase them away. *Let them help you!* And for the rest of us, if you see your church leaders struggling underneath the load of leading God's people, remember this: You have been called to help shoulder their burdens. Pray for them! Offer to help them, and look for opportunities to lighten their load.

Lesson #3: A Lesson from Eldad and Medad: When we are full of God's Spirit, we speak God's *word* and do God's *work* wherever we are, not just at church. Let me ask you two very important questions. First, are you more likely to speak God's word and do His work at church around Christians than you are outside church around non-Christians? If so, you need to follow the example of Eldad and Medad. You need to allow God's Spirit to speak through you regardless of where you are: at church, at home, at work, at school, at the grocery store, at the park, wherever. And just like Moses, you need to allow others to do the same.

My second question to you is this: Do you ever get in the way of God's Spirit when He's working through someone else who is not a part of your church? I'm confident that many of us do. When a Christian from another church knocks on our front door or hands us a tract or communicates his/her Christianity in a way that seems strange to us, our tendency is to say things or do things to shut them up instead of encouraging them in their work for the LORD.

So if the LORD makes it clear to you that He wants to use you to do His work...let Him! *Don't get in His way!* Or if the LORD makes it clear that He wants to use your spouse, your kids, your best friend or your worst enemy to do His work...let Him! *Don't get in His way!* At times we who are Christians act as if we are God's CEOs—as if we have executive authority to overrule any decision God makes that we think is misguided. "Oh, no, LORD! That's a bad idea! Here, let me step in and help You save face. We'd better do this my way instead!"

> At times we act as if we are God's CEOs—as if we have executive authority to overrule any decision God makes that we think is misguided.

Friends, let's not be like Joshua, who wanted to quench the Spirit that the LORD had poured out on Eldad and Medad. When all was said and done, God did exactly what He intended to do: He poured out His Spirit on all seventy of the elders Moses had chosen, regardless of their location. God was *not* in error. He poured out His Spirit as He saw fit, and when Joshua made a move to quench what God was doing, Moses wisely stepped in and ordered Joshua to stand down. We would all do well to tell others—and ourselves—to do the same. When God's Spirit is moving, let Him move. Don't get in the way. Celebrate His Spirit's work in and through His people, and stand down.

The LORD Was Working in Tijuana

The lesson that I learned almost twenty years ago on the outskirts of Tijuana is a lesson that I will never forget. Had I remained at home that week and simply attended the scheduled church services, I would have missed out on a golden opportunity to join Christ in some of His great work. Every Christian needs to gather weekly with other believers for worship, prayer, communion and the study of God's word. But Jesus has commanded us to "go" (Matthew 28:19). And as we do just that—as we obediently *go* and do His work outside the church building—our impact for His Kingdom will be far-reaching, just like that of Eldad and Medad.

CHAPTER 4

Hannah & Peninnah

A Tale of Two Moms

One of the most interesting questions that you can ask a mom is this one: "Why did you want to have children?" If you ask ten different moms this question, you'll likely receive ten different answers. (Come to think of it, if you ask the *same* mom on ten different days, you may *still* get ten different answers.) If you ask this question to a mom in the grocery store when her three-year-old is having a temper tantrum on the floor, she may answer, "I ask myself the same question every day." But if you ask a mom on Mother's Day when the kitchen is a complete mess and the house is filled with the smell of burnt pancakes, she'll likely tell you, "Being a mom is hard, but mornings like this make it all worth it."

If you are a parent, I'd like to ask you the same question: "Why did *you* want to have children?" I encourage you to give it some thought and be honest as you answer it. Maybe you wanted to have kids because you wanted to feel needed. After all, there is no infant on earth more dependent upon its parents than a baby human. Or perhaps you wanted to have kids so that you'd have someone to take care of you when you're old and gray. Personally, I think it would be nice if each of my four girls want to take care of my wife and me when we're seasoned seniors. (And if they can afford to take us on vacations to Hawaii, it'll be even better!)

Maybe, like most parents, you wanted to have kids simply because it is the "normal" thing to do: You grow up. You get married. You have kids. That's just the normal order of things in our culture. (Although in recent decades it has become more common for steps two and three to be switched.) Regardless of *why* you wanted kids in the first place, I'm sure that you want to be a *good* mom or dad. Am I right?

In 1 Samuel 1, God's word tells us a tale of two moms: one good and one…not so good. The not-so-good mom's name was Peninnah (pronounced, **"pi-NIN-uh"**), and the good mom's name was Hannah (pronounced, **"HAN-uh"**). These two moms' stories teach us which parenting *goals* to pursue and which parenting *pitfalls* to avoid.

Two Wives—Bad Idea

The Book of 1 Samuel bridges the gap between two pivotal periods in Israel's history: the Period of the Judges and the Period of the Kings. The Period of the Judges began after Moses' successor, Joshua, led the Israelites into the Promised Land of Canaan. Samuel's life and ministry closed the chapter on the Period of the Judges, and at the same time, as the LORD's chosen priest, he was the one responsible for crowning the first two kings of Israel: King Saul and King David. Samuel is a very important person in the pages of Scripture—lifted up as a hero of the faith in both the Old and New Testaments. In 1 Samuel 1, we are blessed to be able to read the account of how Samuel was born.

> The Book of 1 Samuel bridges the gap between two pivotal periods in Israel's history: the Period of the Judges and the Period of the Kings.

There was a certain man from Ramathaim, a Zuphite from the hill country of Ephraim, whose name was Elkanah son of Jeroham, the son of Elihu, the son of Tohu, the son of Zuph, an Ephraimite. He had two wives; one was called Hannah and the other Peninnah. Peninnah had children, but Hannah had none.

1 Samuel 1:1-2

Samuel's story begins with a man named Elkanah (pronounced, **"el-KAY-nuh"**). We are told that Elkanah had two wives. In his day, this was common practice, but polygamy was not part of God's original plan for marriage. Back in Genesis 2 after God had created Eve, He spoke these powerful prophetic words:

For this reason a man will leave his father and mother and be united to his wife, and they will become one flesh.

Genesis 2:24

Notice that God didn't say that a man will leave his father and *"mothers"* and be united to his *"wives."* God's original plan for marriage was *one* man and *one* woman committed to one another for life. But when the LORD gave the 613 laws to Moses as a rulebook for Israel, He did not specifically *forbid* polygamy. So many Israelite men felt they had a license to marry multiple women. The last verse in the Book of Judges nicely summarizes the prevailing mindset in Elkanah's day:

> God's original plan for marriage was one man and one woman committed to one another for life.

In those days Israel had no king; everyone did as he saw fit.

Judges 21:25

Older English translations translate it this way: "Everyone did what was right in his own eyes." *The Message* paraphrases this verse: "People did whatever they felt like doing."

Sound familiar? *If it feels good, do it!* That was a sad indictment on the Jewish nation in Elkanah's day, and it's just as sad an indictment on the United States of America today. So Elkanah had two wives: Hannah and Peninnah, and according to verse 2, Peninnah had children, but Hannah didn't have a single one. According to verse 4, Peninnah had "sons and daughters," meaning she had at least four kids. But Hannah didn't have any kids because God had "closed her womb." The text here is clear that *the* LORD was the direct cause of her infertility.

Now why on earth would God have closed Hannah's womb when, in her culture, so much of a woman's worth centered around her ability to bear children? Well, we are not told, but it seems clear from the latter part of this chapter that her closed womb was part of God's plan to usher in one of the greatest servants of the LORD in all of Scripture: Samuel. God orchestrated Samuel's birth at the perfect time to carry out a key part of His perfect plan. The LORD seems to have *closed* her womb at a certain time for a purpose, and God would *open* her womb at a certain time for a purpose.

> God orchestrated Samuel's birth at the perfect time to carry out a key part of His perfect plan.

Rival Wives

Now, the plot thickens in verses 3-7.

Year after year this man [Elkanah] went up from his town to worship and sacrifice to the LORD Almighty at Shiloh, where Hophni and Phinehas, the two sons of Eli, were priests of the LORD. Whenever the day came for Elkanah to sacrifice, he would give portions of the meat to his wife Peninnah and to all her sons and daughters. But to Hannah he gave a double portion because he loved her, and the LORD had closed her womb. And because the LORD had closed her womb, her rival kept provoking her in order to irritate her. This went on year after year. Whenever Hannah went up to the house of the LORD, her rival provoked her till she wept and would not eat.

1 Samuel 1:3-7

There are some key words and phrases in these verses that speak volumes. First of all, notice the first three words: "year after year." Hannah's inability to have children persisted "year after year." Peninnah's taunting of Hannah persisted "year after year." The LORD wants us to understand that Hannah's problem was not a short-term problem. It lasted for years!

Also notice this key phrase in verse 5, "But to Hannah [Elkanah] gave a double portion because he loved her." This is a problem we see repeated several times in the Old Testament when men practiced polygamy: Hubby loved one wife more than the other, and that made a bad situation even worse. This is one of many reasons that marrying multiple women is *not* smart.

I don't know if Peninnah was jealous of Hannah because Elkanah loved her more. I don't know if she was just a bully or mean-spirited by nature, but I *do* know that Peninnah was ruthless in her belittling of Hannah, which tore Hannah up inside. Well, what did Elkanah do about the situation? According to verse 8, he intervened by doing some one-on-one intervention with one of his two wives. Unfortunately, Hannah was the one he addressed, not Peninnah.

Elkanah her husband would say to her, "Hannah, why are you weeping? Why don't you eat? Why are you downhearted? Don't I mean more to you than ten sons?"

1 Samuel 1:8

Now, Elkanah meant this last question to be rhetorical. He thought the obvious answer was "Yes." Spoken like a true Casanova, don't you think? *Who needs a son when you have... ME!* Well, Elkanah was a very faithful and loving husband to Hannah, but that didn't stop her from wanting a son. This cycle of Peninnah taunting Hannah to the point of tears repeated itself year after year as Elkanah and his family traveled to Shiloh for the annual sacrifice. But something changed one year according to verses 9-11.

Hannah Cries Out to the LORD

Once when they had finished eating and drinking in Shiloh, Hannah stood up. Now Eli the priest was sitting on a chair by the doorpost of the LORD's temple. In bitterness of soul Hannah wept much and prayed to the LORD. And she made a vow, saying, "O LORD Almighty, if You will only look upon Your servant's misery and remember me, and not forget Your servant but give her a son, then I will give him to the LORD for all the days of his life and no razor will ever be used on his head."

1 Samuel 1:9-11

This particular year Hannah was bound and determined to do something about her miserable situation. She was powerless to open her own womb, but she was convinced that what was *impossible* for her was *possible* with God. So she stood up after the meal had been eaten, entered the tabernacle and began weeping and praying to the LORD. And she made a vow to Him. She promised the LORD that if He opened her womb and blessed her with a son, she would do two significant things:

#1: She would give the boy back to the LORD to serve Him throughout his lifetime.

#2: She would set him apart from birth as a Nazirite. (That's what she means when she says, "No razor will be used on his head.")

A Nazirite vow is explained in detail in Numbers 6. In short, the vow involved a *separation* and *dedication* to the LORD for a specific period of time. In some cases, as with Samson, the vow lasted one's *entire* lifetime. Aside from refraining from haircuts, a Nazirite was also forbidden from eating or drinking grape products. And he could never approach a dead body.

Just as the LORD had set Samson apart from before birth as a Nazirite, Hannah promised to set her own son apart as a Nazirite from before birth. She made this vow and continued praying fervently. She prayed so fervently, in fact, that the high priest Eli was convinced that she was drunk (verse 14). It seems that fervent, heartfelt prayer was so sparse in those days that even the high priest didn't recognize it. (And I fear that the same could be said of Christ's Church in America today.)

> It seems that fervent, heartfelt prayer was so sparse in those days that even the high priest didn't recognize it.

In verses 15-16 Hannah respectfully informed Eli that he was mistaken about her being drunk. She explained: "I was pouring out my soul to the LORD," to which Eli responded with a word of blessing for Hannah. And we read some marvelous words in verse 18. As Hannah left the temple, "her face was no longer downcast." *The Message* paraphrases it this way: "her face [was] radiant."

It sounds to me like Hannah had faith that the LORD was going to answer her prayer. Wouldn't you agree? And God *did* answer her prayer.

> The LORD remembered her. So in the course of time Hannah conceived and gave birth to a son. She named him Samuel, saying, "Because I asked the LORD for him."
>
> 1 Samuel 1:19b-20

The name Samuel sounds like the Hebrew word for "heard of God." The LORD had heard Hannah's humble prayer, and He had seen her pain-filled tears. And as He has done so often throughout history, He responded with a miracle. God opened Hannah's womb and blessed her with a baby boy. And since the LORD had done what Hannah had asked of Him, she was bound and determined to do exactly what she had promised to do. She was going to set him apart for the LORD and give her boy back to Him. Consider the remarkable actions and words of this godly woman in the final verses of the chapter:

> After he was weaned, she took the boy with her, young as he was, along with a three-year-old bull, an ephah of flour and a skin of wine, and brought him to the house of the LORD at Shiloh. When they had slaughtered the bull they brought the boy to Eli, and she said to him, "As surely as you live, my LORD, I am the woman who stood here beside you praying to the LORD. I prayed for this child, and the LORD has granted me what I asked of Him. So now I give him to the LORD. For his whole life he will be given over to the LORD." And he worshiped the LORD there.
>
> 1 Samuel 1:24-28

In Hannah's day a child could be weaned anytime between the ages of two and six years old. So Samuel could have been as young as two when Hannah fulfilled her promise to the LORD, bringing him back to the tabernacle to serve Him all the days of his life. Wow! What a remarkably strong woman Hannah was!

5 Life Lessons

There's no doubt that Hannah and Peninnah had a *few* things in common. For starters, they were both Jewish. And they were both women married to the same man. It also seems clear that they both *wanted* to have children. But other than that, these moms were as different as night and day. These moms were complete opposites in at least five different ways. As we take a brief look at each of these five differences, I encourage you to ask yourself: Am I more like Peninnah or more like Hannah?

Life Lesson #1: Peninnah was mean and hard-hearted, while Hannah was kind and tender-hearted. Parents, how are you doing in this area? Moms, when you interact with your kids, are you more like a drill sergeant or more like a loving teacher and coach? Dads, do you guide your kids with an iron fist or with a tender touch? Your kids don't need you to be blowing your top and storming through the house like Attila the Hun. Moms, your kids don't need to see you being mean and disrespectful to other adults including your husband. The Apostle Peter reminds you of the power of a woman's gentle spirit.

> Your beauty should not come from outward adornment, such as braided hair and the wearing of gold jewelry and fine clothes. Instead, it should be that of your inner self,

the unfading beauty of a gentle and quiet spirit, which is of great worth in God's sight.

1 Peter 3:3-4

Peninnah may have been a very attractive woman on the outside, but what poured out of her mouth revealed the deeper truth: She was very ugly on the inside. So parents, don't be mean and hard-hearted like Peninnah. Be kind and tender-hearted like Hannah.

Life Lesson #2: Peninnah used her kids to bring *herself* glory, while Hannah offered her only son to bring *God* glory. Parents, how are you doing in this area? Peninnah is a classic example of a mom who was a mom for all the wrong reasons. We don't have any indication in 1 Samuel that Peninnah had any noble motives for wanting children. No indication is given that she wanted to teach them, invest herself in them or love them. She seems to have wanted to have kids simply because they made *her* look good.

> Peninnah seems to have wanted to have kids simply because they made her look good. Hannah, however, wanted to have a son who would make the LORD look good.

But Hannah's motives were godly. She wanted to have a son who would make *the* LORD look good. She wanted to have a son who would bring *God* glory. And when she received Samuel, there isn't any indication that she said, "Neener, neener, neener" to Peninnah. She just humbly and lovingly prepared him to be given back to the LORD.

I want to show you two verses that I believe to be among the most inspirational verses in the whole Bible about mothering. In the next chapter (1 Samuel 2) we read these wonderful words:

Samuel was ministering before the LORD—a boy wearing a linen ephod. Each year his mother made him a little robe and took it to him when she went up with her husband to offer the annual sacrifice.

1 Samuel 2:18-19

You can tell that Hannah loved her son and was proud to have him serving the LORD at such a young age. She took so much joy in making a new, little robe for him each year and hand-delivering it to him. Hannah is a wonderful example of a loving mother.

Life Lesson #3: Peninnah went through the motions of worship, but Hannah poured out her soul in worship and prayer to the LORD. Parents, how are you doing in this area? When it's time for a worship service, do you, like Peninnah, tag along with the rest of your family and go through the motions of singing, giving an offering and listening to the pastor's message, or do you, like Hannah, pour out your soul in worship and prayer to the LORD? Moms and dads, your kids are watching you. If you just go through the motions of worship, your kids will too. But if they witness you on a weekly basis humbly crying out to the LORD in prayer and worshiping Him with joy and enthusiasm, there's a very strong likelihood that they'll follow in your footsteps.

Life Lesson #4: Peninnah didn't feel the need to lean on God, but Hannah was *desperate* for God. Consider this: If all of our prayers are prayed with perfect composure, then we aren't truly desperate for the LORD. I'm not saying that we need to try to look drunk or crazy when we pray. Jesus taught against praying showy prayers. But the simple fact of the matter is: When we cry out to God in desperation, we are not going to look composed.

If a husband is begging his wife not to leave him, he will not look composed. If a thirsty child is begging her mom for a drink of water, she will not look composed. And if you are desperate for

God to break an addiction in your life or lift you out of financial ruin or heal you of cancer, you're not going to look composed when *you* pray.

Parents, how are you doing in this area? Do you, like Peninnah, lean on your *own* understanding when you face decisions and lean on your *own* strength when times get tough, or are you, like Hannah, desperate for God?

One of the classic books on prayer was written by O. Hallesby, one of Norway's most loved devotional writers of the mid-20th century. He wrote these inspiring words about the power of desperate prayer:

> Prayer and helplessness are inseparable. Only those who are helpless can truly pray...Listen, my friend! Your helplessness is your best prayer. It calls from your heart to the heart of God with greater effect than all your uttered pleas. He hears it from the very moment that you are seized with helplessness, and He becomes actively engaged at once in hearing and answering the prayer of your helplessness.[2]

Parents, your words, your sacrifices and your example impact your children more than your realize. But I can also tell you that your greatest impact on your kids will be through your helpless prayers for them. When you turn to God in desperation and say: "LORD, I can't soften my child's hard heart; I can't get through to him. There's nothing more that I can do. LORD, touch him. LORD, change her. LORD, save my child!" Moms and dads, it's then and only then that you will exert the greatest impact on your child. There is no power in the universe

"Listen, my friend! Your helplessness is your best prayer. It calls from your heart to the heart of God with greater effect than all your uttered pleas." – O. Hallesby

like the power God unleashes in response to a desperate parent's prayers.

Life Lesson #5: Peninnah's greatest joy was in *keeping* her children, while Hannah's greatest joy was in *giving* her child back to God. Parents, how are you doing in this area? At this point I need to toot my own mom's horn. My mom has told me time and time again over the years of my life that she never thought of me as *hers*. From the day I was born she didn't see me as "her boy" but as "God's boy." Friends, that's a very refreshing perspective in this day and age when it's all about me, myself and I.

Do you remember the scene from "Finding Nemo" when Nemo's dad and Dori have finally made it to Sydney, Australia? They're within a few miles of where the lost clownfish Nemo is. Their search and rescue operation is almost complete, but there are dozens of obstacles still in their way...namely, a flock of seagulls. Nemo's dad and Dori are being chased by dozens of seagulls who all want fish for dinner, and the gulls are all screeching: "MINE! MINE! MINE! MINE! MINE! MINE!"

Think about this: Every one of those sea gulls could have been named *Peninnah*. Moms, don't be like the sea gulls. Don't be like Peninnah. That boy that you gave birth to is "*God's* boy," and that girl that you carried in your womb is "*God's* girl." They are entrusted to you, but they are simply on loan from God. They are His. So view them as such.

> From the very first day that you receive each child, you should begin giving him/her back to God.

Dads, the same goes for you. You have the privilege of rearing God's boys and girls, but from the very first day that you receive each child, you should begin giving him/her back to God. Oh, the LORD will most likely never ask you to drop him/her off at the local church building to be raised by the pastor, but He *does* ask you to *teach* your children His word, *lead* them to Christ and *train* them to serve Him. (Come to think of it, in some ways, dropping them at the church might be easier!)

So do you spend time in God's word with your kids each day? *You should.* Do you take your children with you to church each week? *You need to.* Do you lead your kids in the direction that God would have them go, not the direction *you* would have them go? *You must.* Regardless of *why* you wanted to have kids in the first place, the LORD has called you to *receive them* as a gift from His hand and, just like Hannah, *prepare them* to serve Him.

CHAPTER 5

Eliab Son of Jesse

Tall, Dark, Handsome...and Rejected

When I was in grade school, I loved to play kickball. And when it came time to pick teams, there was nothing deep or profound about my method of choosing teammates. I didn't care if a kid was a Christian or atheist; I didn't care if he made A's or F's. I didn't even care if he terrorized his little sister at home. All I cared about was the answer to one simple question: Could the kid play kickball? If he could kick hard and run fast and catch fly balls, that's all I needed to know. The kid could have the IQ of a tree slug and the temperament of Genghis Khan. I didn't care. I only cared about one thing: winning! So if Genghis could help me win, I'd choose him in a heartbeat.

It's human nature, I suppose: choosing muscles over manners, popularity over principle, charisma over character. As a rule of thumb, we cheer for our favorite teams and our favorite players in the NBA, NFL and MLB regardless of how deplorable their behavior is off the court or field. Many of our favorite athletes are egomaniacs who are abusive husbands, deadbeat dads and could care less about the things of God. But as long as they perform on the court or on the field, we lift them up as our heroes.

And for those of you who don't care much about sports, do I even need to mention our politicians? Suffice it to say that we ignore a lot of immoral behavior in our politicians as long as they advance *our* causes and serve *our* needs. Let's face it: When it comes to picking heroes to save us or leaders to lead us, we tend to be pretty shallow.

But not God. He looks deeper. He looks past a person's height, build and profile. He doesn't care if you're photogenic, and He doesn't care if you're physically coordinated. He doesn't care if your IQ is 75 or 175, if you were born in a palace or in the projects. He doesn't care if you're a registered Republican, Democrat or Independent. When the LORD looks for a hero to inspire us or a leader to lead us, He looks right through all the surface stuff. He finds His leaders by examining the heart.

> Let's face it: When it comes to picking heroes to save us or leaders to lead us, we tend to be pretty shallow.

That's how the LORD chose the greatest king of Israel, King David. By most standards David was a "nobody" until God transformed him into a "somebody." He wasn't the biggest, strongest or best-looking teenager in town. He had never won a "Who's Who" award or been voted "most likely to succeed." But the LORD saw something in David that nobody else saw. So He plucked David out of the sheep fields and dropped him in front of a nine-foot giant named Goliath. And the teenager everyone had overlooked became an instant hero.

We all know David, but most of us would be hard-pressed to recall the name of David's oldest brother. His name was Eliab son of Jesse (pronounced, **"il-I-uhb"**), and we are introduced to him in 1 Samuel 16.

The Rejected King

Samuel had been serving as Israel's judge and priest for over forty years. And the most recent twenty years or so had been particularly challenging. In 1 Samuel 8:4-5, we read that all of Israel's elders approached Samuel and asked him to appoint a king to lead their nation. The people of Israel wanted to have a human king just like the other nations. They weren't content to have the LORD as their king.

So, after giving the people a clear warning of the hardships that a human king would bring, Samuel did what the people asked of him. He gave them a king: Saul son of Kish. He was big. He was tall. Saul just *looked* like a king. We're told in 1 Samuel 9:2 that he was a head taller than other men. Because of his impressive physical characteristics, most of the Israelites were ecstatic. At long last, the king they'd been hoping for had arrived!

Unfortunately, Saul's character wasn't nearly as tall as his stature. Although he was a humble and obedient king at first, he couldn't disguise his flawed character for very long. He disobeyed God's commands on multiple occasions, and his pride kept him from humbly repenting after doing so. By the time we get to 1 Samuel 16, the LORD had already rejected Saul as king of Israel. God had made it clear to Samuel that the next king would be a man whose heart chased after God's heart (1 Samuel 13:14).

As chapter 15 draws to a close, Samuel was in his hometown of Ramah having a pity party. Samuel was a godly man, but it seems he was trying to change God's mind about rejecting Saul. But it was too late for that; God had already made up His mind. Thus, Samuel was wasting his tears and squandering his talents on Saul. To use Jesus' words, Samuel was "throwing his pearls to pigs" (Matthew 7:6).

The Parade of Sons

The LORD said to Samuel, "How long will you mourn for Saul, since I have rejected him as king over Israel? Fill your horn with oil and be on your way; I am sending you to Jesse of Bethlehem. I have chosen one of his sons to be king."

1 Samuel 16:1

A certain son of Jesse was God's choice for the next king of Israel. Samuel's job was to find him and anoint him with oil, declaring him to be king. The LORD's point is clear: "Samuel, now is not the time to be grieving over the old king. Now is the time to be rejoicing over the new king." So after a few moments of grumbling, Samuel did what the LORD instructed him to do. He filled his horn with anointing oil and hit the road. Bethlehem or bust!

When Samuel rolled into town, Bethlehem's elders were scared to death. After all, their little country town was not on the normal stopping route for the most powerful priest in the country. When Samuel walked into town, they figured they'd done something *really bad*!

To understand their fears, imagine three squad cars pulling into your driveway with brakes squealing and sirens blaring. Your first thought wouldn't be that they were making a light-hearted social call, would it? "Maybe the deputies are running low on coffee, and they need me to top off their cups." I don't think so! When the cops are pounding on your front door, you figure someone in your family is in *really big trouble*.

Well, Samuel assured the elders that nobody was in trouble. He asked them to consecrate themselves and join him for a sacrifice. And that's where our mystery man, Eliab son of Jesse, comes onto the scene.

When [Jesse and his sons] arrived, Samuel saw Eliab and thought, "Surely the LORD's anointed stands here before the LORD."

1 Samuel 16:6

Although King Saul had served as a clear illustration that good looks and a strong frame don't make a man a great king, as Eliab walked past Samuel, the old prophet got caught up in the moment. Maybe it was the fact that Eliab was the eldest son. Maybe it was the way his younger brothers fell in line behind him out of admiration and respect. Maybe it was his rugged good looks: tall, dark and handsome. He looked every bit as stately as Saul had looked when Samuel had first anointed *him* as king. Samuel took a good, hard look at Eliab and said to himself, "Surely the LORD's anointed stands here before the LORD."

As he stared at Eliab, Samuel must have had a glimmer in his eye and a grin above his chin. "Just look at him," Samuel must have thought, "He's perfect! He's got kingly stature, kingly hair, kingly biceps and a kingly voice. He's even got a kingly Orbit smile." We're not told the specifics. All we know is this: Samuel was impressed with what he saw as Eliab walked by, and he was convinced that Eliab was "the one."

> "Just look at him," Samuel must have thought, "He's perfect! He's got kingly stature, kingly hair, kingly biceps. He's even got a kingly Orbit smile."

But before Samuel had a chance to pop the cork off his horn and start pouring oil on Eliab's head, God stopped Samuel in his tracks. He spoke to Samuel's spirit, sharing with him some of the most insightful verses in all Scripture about what God looks for in a leader.

But the LORD said to Samuel, "Do not consider his appearance or his height, for I have rejected him. The LORD does not look at the outward appearance, but the LORD looks at the heart."

1 Samuel 16:7

Let's break this verse down and take a closer look. "Do not consider his appearance or his height, for I have rejected him." Translation: It doesn't matter how good he looks. It doesn't matter how handsome he is, how tall he is or how many women swoon when he walks into a crowded room. If God hasn't chosen him, that's all that matters. Israel's next king wouldn't be chosen by popular vote. In fact, there wouldn't be a vote at all. The next king would be *God's* choice.

"The LORD does not look at the things man looks at. Man looks at the outward appearance, but the LORD looks at the heart." Translation: When people look for a hero, we tend to look only skin deep. To verify this is true, simply visit a school playground at recess or a neighborhood park on a weekend. Watch how teams are chosen for a pickup basketball or touch football game. Kids choose teammates the same way that *I* chose them in grade school. Kickball, anyone?

Now, when we speak of the LORD looking at the heart, it *sounds* great, but what exactly does it mean? Simply put, it means that God inspects the *source* of our words and actions. God probes our motives; God examines our deepest cravings and passions. God looks at our *internal* morality, which is always a clearer reflection of the real us than is our *outward* morality. God is able to look right through us to see what we *really* believe, what we *really* care about, what we *really* love and what we *really* hate. I can say all day long to you, "I love God with all my heart, and I hate sin." But God searches inside me to see if I really mean it or if I'm just putting on a show to impress you. God looks at the heart.

Throughout the Bible we find this to be true. God looks at the human heart and does His most life-changing work inside it. And the greatest followers of Jesus Christ always let Him. Consider this inspiring truth from 2 Chronicles.

> For the eyes of the LORD range throughout the earth to strengthen those whose hearts are fully committed to Him.
>
> 2 Chronicles 16:9

The LORD specifically chose David to be the next king because He looked at David's very core and saw that he was "a man after [God's] own heart" (1 Samuel 13:14). And when King David was about to die, he gave this charge to his son Solomon:

> "Above all else, guard your heart, for it is the wellspring of life."
> (Proverbs 4:23)

> "And you, my son Solomon, acknowledge the God of your father, and serve Him with wholehearted devotion and with a willing mind, for the LORD searches every heart and understands every motive behind the thoughts. If you seek Him, He will be found by you; but if you forsake Him, He will reject you forever.
>
> 1 Chronicles 28:9

The LORD Himself spoke these words through the prophet Jeremiah:

> You will seek Me and find Me when you seek Me with all your heart.
>
> Jeremiah 29:13

When we have hearts that truly love God and truly hunger and thirst for doing what is right—what pleases Him—He will know it. And we will follow in the footsteps of the psalmist:

I have hidden Your word in my heart that I might not sin against You.

Psalm 119:11

We will also heed the counsel of Solomon:

Trust in the LORD with all your heart and lean not on your own understanding.

Proverbs 3:5

Above all else, guard your heart, for it is the wellspring of life.

Proverbs 4:23

Honestly, this is just the tip of the iceberg when it comes to what the Bible says about the priority of our hearts to God. When it comes down to it, a person's Christianity may look great on the outside, but God is looking past what *we* see to what only *He* can see. So I ask you: How's your heart today? You may be able to hide the truth even from those who know you best, but you can't hide the truth from God. He sees your heart, and He knows it completely.

The LORD looked at Eliab, and He didn't see a knight in shining armor. He saw a hard and corrupt heart. So God rejected him along with his other six brothers who were in attendance at the sacrifice. The LORD looked past the feast and found His chosen king out in the sheep fields. God looked at David, and He didn't see the runt of the litter, a measly little shepherd boy who wasn't good for anything other than watching a few dozen sheep. The LORD saw a soft heart that chased hard after God. And more than anything else, that's what God was looking for in Israel's next hero. That's what He was looking for in Israel's next leader. So in God's perfect wisdom, David was the *perfect* choice to become king.

Eliab Returns

Eliab comes onto the scene one more time in 1 Samuel. In the very next chapter, 1 Samuel 17, we find one of the most famous stories in the whole Bible: the story of David and Goliath. But before David stood on the battlefield and faced Goliath with a sling and five stones, he asked the Israelite soldiers about Goliath and what reward King Saul would give the soldier who killed him. David's oldest brother Eliab heard David asking these questions, and he was furious.

> When Eliab, David's oldest brother, heard him speaking with the men, he burned with anger at him and asked, "Why have you come down here? And with whom did you leave those few sheep in the desert? I know how conceited you are and how wicked your heart is; you came down only to watch the battle."
>
> 1 Samuel 17:28

As the LORD was setting the scene for the mighty giant to fall, Eliab showed himself to be the pitiful man that he was. God had rejected Eliab because of his *wicked* heart, and He had accepted David because of his *pure* heart. Yet here Eliab accused David of having a wicked heart and implied that he himself had a pure one. Eliab could have done great things for God's kingdom, but his heart wasn't right. So he disappeared off the pages of Scripture after this verse as a man who was physically impressive but spiritually bankrupt. For the past 3,000-plus years God's followers have been eternally grateful to David for ignoring his older brother Eliab's criticism. Instead, he took to the field that day in the power of God and slew the giant with a single stone in his sling.

Although Samuel had served as Israel's primary religious leader for decades, he had somehow failed to internalize this reality: If a man's heart isn't right before God, he is disqualified for leadership in God's Kingdom. Period.

To God the heart is the most important part of the body. If one's heart is right, one's *thoughts* will be right. If a person's heart is right, his *words* will be right. If a man's heart is right, his *actions* will be right.

> To God the heart is the most important part of the body. If one's heart is right, one's thoughts will be right. If a person's heart is right, his words and actions will be right.

Although Israel had dozens of kings over a period of more than 450 years, King David was, without a doubt, Israel's greatest king. And his greatness didn't stem from his good looks, his musical talents, his tremendous leadership abilities or even from his ability to so effectively wield a sword. His greatness stemmed from one part of his body. You guessed it…his heart.

3 Life Lessons

Life Lesson #1: A Lesson from Samuel: Do what the LORD says. Period. To Samuel, it sounded like suicide for him to run off and anoint the next king while King Saul was still on the throne. But Samuel wasn't lord of his own life. The LORD was his Lord. So he obeyed. According to verse 4, "Samuel did what the LORD said." Can the same be said about you? Do you obey God's word, even when it sounds crazy to do so? Do you do what the LORD says? If not, He's not really your Lord. Don't forget Jesus' words:

"Why do you call me, 'Lord, Lord,' and do not do what I say?"

Luke 6:46

"If you love me, you will obey what I command."

John 14:15

Life Lesson #2: A Lesson from God: The LORD is not fooled by our masks. He sees right through them to our hearts. So guard your heart and ask Him to search it and clean it up. This account of David's selection and Eliab's rejection is a powerful reminder that God is most concerned with the condition of our hearts. One of my favorite psalms is Psalm 139, within which David praises God for being his Creator who knows him inside and out. And David ends Psalm 139 with this wonderful prayer of petition that I have prayed for myself many times over the years:

Search me, O God, and know my heart; test me and know my anxious thoughts. See if there is any offensive way in me, and lead me in the way everlasting.

Psalm 139:23-24

We would all do well to pray this same prayer—and mean it. David knew that the LORD already knew his heart. So he humbly partnered with God in the process, in essence asking God to reveal to him anything in his heart that was *not* right—anything that was offensive to God—so that together the LORD and David could eradicate it and make his heart right before God. Can you see why David was called "a man after God's own heart"?

Lesson #3: A Lesson From Eliab: We would be wise to spend *less* time judging others' hearts and *more* time making

sure our own hearts are right before God. Friends, Christianity is a process...a process of moving from death to life, from sin to sanctification, from separation *from* God to closeness *with* God. And this process can not be carried out without a dynamic partnership between you and the Holy Spirit of Jesus Christ working inside you. Sure, the Christians around you are rough around the edges, but so are you! Before you can help them with the specks of sin in their eyes, you have to work with the Holy Spirit to deal with the plank in your own eye (see Matthew 7:3).

Over time the Holy Spirit will work with you to disinfect your foul mouth, align your priorities and improve your bad behavior. But most of all, the Holy Spirit will work on your heart, because your heart

> Over time the Holy Spirit will work with you to disinfect your foul mouth, align your priorities and improve your bad behavior. But most of all, the Holy Spirit will work on your heart.

is "the wellspring of life" (Proverbs 4:23). The Holy Spirit will be working patiently and methodically day by day to replace your heart of stone with a heart of flesh, to make your dirty heart clean, and to transform your *selfish* heart into a *selfless* heart. He is gently bringing each of us to a place where we can love as Christ loves, loving God with all our heart, mind, soul and strength.

The LORD desires to do open heart surgery on you. I urge you to let Him. Don't get in His way. He can already see your heart, so why not allow Him to *transform* it while He's *inspecting* it? If you truly desire God to transform your heart today, I encourage you to join me in praying a prayer like this one:

A Suggested Prayer:

Father, give me a heart like David's, a heart that loves You more than anything or anyone, a heart that is clean and produces clean motives, clean thoughts, clean words and clean actions. Father, give me a heart like David's: a heart that follows hard after You and loves the things that You love and hates the things that You hate. Father, give me a heart like David's: a heart that You look for in a leader of Your people, a heart that You look for when Your eyes go back and forth around the earth to find someone whose heart is fully committed to You. Father, give me a heart like David's. In Jesus' name, Amen!

CHAPTER 6

Shimei Son of Gera

He Was a Royal Pain in the Neck

When I was in grade school I was convinced that one of the boys in my class was the meanest kid in the world. (I'll just call him "Jimmy.") In fourth or fifth grade Jimmy swung his jacket and struck me next to my eye with the jacket's metal zipper. As my face began to throb in pain, I ran off and hid inside an oversized tire that was on the playground. Did Jimmy come over and apologize? Oh no! He hung over the side of the tire and cackled, "Oh! Look at the crybaby! Ha! Ha! Ha!"

When it came down to it, Jimmy had no reservations about name-calling, cutting in line, pushing, shoving or throwing his weight around. Now, as a child I had a knack for getting along with other kids who could be classified as "EGR" (Extra Grace Required), but I really couldn't *stand* that kid! He was a big bully who, if things didn't drastically change, was going to end up in juvenile hall. I hope and pray that he made the necessary changes, changes that he could only make if Jesus Christ was in the driver's seat of his life. With Jimmy calling his own shots, his life was headed nowhere fast.

In elementary school Jimmy was my Shimei (pronounced, "**SHIM-ee-i**"). In junior high, Anthony was my Shimei. Over the years, I've had a number of other Shimeis in my life. I bet you have too. You may even have a Shimei or two in your life right now.

In 2 Samuel 16, we can learn some valuable lessons from David about how to handle a Shimei when he comes our way. Most of us will have to deal with many more Shimeis in the years ahead. So King David's example will be invaluable to you.

> Over the years you've had a number of Shimeis in your life. You may even have one or two Shimeis in your life right now.

Things Weren't Going So Well for King David

When David faced Goliath on the battlefield, he was a young man—possibly still a teenager. But by the time we reach 2 Samuel 16, around forty years had passed. David's hair had grayed, and he had about thirty years of experience under his belt as king. But King David was facing one of the toughest challenges of his life. His own son, Absalom, had staged a coup to march on Jerusalem and steal the throne from him.

Absalom was so ambitious to become king that he was prepared to kill his own dad along with anyone else who stood in his way. But David was not prepared to lift a finger to harm his own son, so he gathered his wives and kids and fled Jerusalem. David quickly made his way out of the city, over the Mount of Olives, and was making his way down the mountain pass.

Bahurim was a town close to the town of Bethany where one thousand years later Jesus would raise Lazarus from the dead. As David, his family and the troops with him approached the town of Bahurim, one of the late King Saul's relatives came out of the town to intercept David and his men. His name was Shimei son of Gera, and he was a human wrecking ball. Shimei spotted David fleeing Jerusalem and proceeded to come out of his town and start cursing David up and down.

> As King David approached Bahurim, a man from the same clan as Saul's family came out from there. His name was Shimei son of Gera, and he cursed as he came out. He pelted David and all the king's officials with stones, though all the troops and the special guard were on David's right and left. As he cursed, Shimei said, "Get out, get out, you man of blood, you scoundrel! The LORD has repaid you for all the blood you shed in the household of Saul, in whose place you have reigned. The LORD has handed the kingdom over to your son Absalom. You have come to ruin because you are a man of blood!"
>
> 2 Samuel 16:5-8

It seems clear that Shimei hated David with a passion and had been harboring a grudge against him for some time. In his anger Shimei didn't just shower David with four-letter words; he also showered him and all his officials with stones. These weren't little pebbles either; some of these rocks could have knocked David silly if they had hit him in the head.

According to verse 6, the troops formed a wall of soldiers around David to protect him from attack. But even with the soldiers surrounding him, David and his officials were still getting pelted. So you can imagine what these soldiers and guards must have done. They must have made a tight formation and lifted their shields over their heads to form a defensive barrier over David, protecting him from the descending rocks.

But nothing could shield David's ears from Shimei's verbal barrage. Shimei yelled, "Get out, get out, you man of blood, you scoundrel!" *The Message* paraphrases Shimei's bellowing this way: "Get lost, get lost, you butcher, you hellhound!" And according to verse 7, Shimei spoke these words "as he cursed." Do you know what that means? It means that what we have recorded here in verse 7 is a PG-rated excerpt from Shimei's R-rated curses. In today's terms, Shimei was dropping "F-bombs" and other four-letter words like you wouldn't believe.

Now, once we get past the shock of what this man was saying and doing to King David, we have to ask ourselves: "What on earth was Shimei talking about?" Was he just pulling slanderous accusations out of the air, or did he really believe that David was a man of blood? Did he really believe that David was a butcher and scoundrel? And the answer is: Yes, he did.

> What we have recorded in 2 Samuel 16:7 is a PG-rated excerpt from Shimei's R-rated curses.

But why? We know David as the "man after God's own heart." We know David as the harp-playing singer and poet. We know David as the man who was a warrior for God, not for the enemy. We know David as a man of integrity. How could there be any substance to Shimei's accusations?

David Wasn't Everyone's Hero

Before we explore the answer to this question, let's look again at what Shimei said in verse 8:

> "The LORD has repaid you for all the blood you shed in the household of Saul, in whose place you have reigned. The LORD has handed the kingdom over to your son Absalom. You have come to ruin because you are a man of blood!"
>
> 2 Samuel 16:8

Well, to understand what on earth Shimei was talking about, we have to go back about fourteen chapters in 2 Samuel. Forty years earlier when David left the battlefield carrying Goliath's head, he became an instant hero in Israel. Within a few short months the Israelite women began singing the refrain, "Saul has slain his thousands but David his tens of thousands." To the Israelites who had grown sick and tired of those pesky Philistines, David was an answer to their prayers. He was the hero for whom they had prayed. To them he was like Ulysses S. Grant, Dwight D. Eisenhower and Rambo rolled into one with a dash of Elvis for good measure.

David was Israel's hero, but not everyone was sending him fan mail. Even at the height of his popularity, David had plenty of enemies, including King Saul, who was insanely jealous of him. On two occasions Saul tried to pin David to the palace wall with his spear.

It was some ten years after his battle with Goliath that King Saul and his son Jonathan died in battle, and the LORD instructed David to go to Hebron where he would be anointed king for the second time. But the rest of Israel didn't recognize David as their new king. While David was being coronated as king in Hebron, Abner, the commander of Saul's army, took Saul's son Ish-Bosheth and anointed *him* as king of Israel.

And so began a seven-year power struggle between David's loyal followers and Ish-Bosheth's loyal followers. King David came out on top, but in the process of winning the struggle, things got ugly. David's general Joab killed Ish-Bosheth's general in cold blood. And a few days later, two of Ish-Bosheth's soldiers murdered Ish-Bosheth. King David strongly condemned both of these murders, but it didn't stop members of Saul's family from blaming and resenting David.

Grains of Truth in the Accusations?

With this historical background in mind, let's take a closer look at Shimei's accusations against David.

Verse 7: "you man of blood"—Is there any truth in this accusation? Was David a man of blood? As the captain of the guard in Saul's army, he certainly was. Even God Himself told David that he was a warrior who shed blood (1 Chronicles 28:3). That's the primary reason that God didn't want David to be the one to build the temple. God wanted a man of peace to build His temple. Although Shimei mistakenly believed that David had shed innocent blood in Saul's household, his accusation was true in a general sense: David *was* a man of blood.

Verse 7: "you scoundrel" (more literally, "you worthless fellow")—Is there any truth in this accusation? Well, David's worth was a matter of opinion. But at this point David probably *felt* pretty worthless. His son was trying to kill him, he was running for his life, and this Shimei yahoo was only adding to his misery.

Verse 8: "The LORD has repaid you for all the blood you shed in the household of Saul, in whose place you have reigned."—Is there any truth in this accusation? In this case, no. David's conduct was above reproach when it came to Saul. Even though Saul had tried to murder David time and time again, David refused to lift a finger to harm Saul. And though most kings in David's day would have killed the sons of the prior king, David did the opposite. He searched for children of Saul so that he could protect them and show them kindness.

Verse 8: "The LORD has handed the kingdom over to your son Absalom."—Is there any substance to this claim? No. Although it must have seemed to be the case as David was fleeing the capital city, God had done no such thing. Absalom would never become king of Israel.

Verse 8: "You have come to ruin because you are a man of blood!"—Is there any truth in this claim? In this case, some. Shimei was overstating things. David hadn't "come to ruin," but this misery that he was experiencing was in fact a direct result of his own sin.

2 Samuel 11 documents the details of the lowest point in David's life. David got out of his bed one night and took a little stroll on the palace roof. As he gazed across the neighborhood, his eyes beheld a beautiful woman bathing on her terrace. Her name was Bathsheba. David allowed an accidental glance to turn into a gawking stare. David lusted after Bathsheba in his heart, and his lust set in motion a negative chain of events. David committed adultery with her, got her pregnant and staged a cover-up that included the murder of Bathsheba's husband, Uriah, on the battlefield.

And in 2 Samuel 12, God sent the prophet Nathan to confront David about his sin. He told David very plainly what God's punishment was going to be for the evil that he had done.

> "Why did you despise the word of the LORD by doing what is evil in His eyes? You struck down Uriah the Hittite with the sword and took his wife to be your own. You killed him with the sword of the Ammonites. Now, therefore, the sword will never depart from your house, because you despised me and took the wife of Uriah the Hittite to be your own. This is what the LORD says: 'Out of your own household I am going to bring calamity upon you. Before your very eyes I will take your wives and give them to one who is close to you, and he will lie with your wives in broad daylight. You did it in secret, but I will do this thing in broad daylight before all Israel.'" Then David said to Nathan, "I have sinned against the LORD."
>
> 2 Samuel 12:9-13a

Here's the sad truth of the matter: What we read in 2 Samuel 16 is the perfect fulfillment of Nathan's prophecy in chapter 12. David had to flee Jerusalem because God had allowed Absalom to arise out of David's own house to "bring calamity upon" him. And Shimei's curses and stone-throwing were all part of this calamity.

> "Do not be deceived: God cannot be mocked. A man reaps what he sows."
> Galatians 6:7

In the latter part of 2 Samuel 16, we find the disturbing fulfillment of the rest of Nathan's prophecy about David. When Absalom rolled into Jerusalem, he pitched a tent on top of the palace and proceeded to have intercourse with all ten of David's concubines who had remained behind at the palace. David's affair with Bathsheba was *private* and behind closed doors, but Absalom's ten affairs were *public*, on the roof in broad daylight.

So the bottom line is this: David reaped what he had sown. David had sown seeds of *adultery* with another man's wife, and now David's own son was committing adultery with David's concubines. He had sown seeds of *murder* with Bathsheba's husband, and now David's own son was trying to murder him. The Apostle Paul gives us this powerful reminder in his letter to the Galatians:

> Do not be deceived: God cannot be mocked. A man reaps what he sows. The one who sows to please the sinful nature, from that nature will reap destruction; the one who sows to please the Spirit, from the Spirit will reap eternal life.
>
> Galatians 6:7-8

David understood this biblical truth, which explains his response to Shimei in the next few verses.

David's Response

Verse 6 makes it clear that it wasn't just David who was suffering the annoyance of a dirt-and-stone shower. His officials and traveling companions were getting pelted as well, and they, like David, were getting pretty annoyed by it. In verse 9, one of David's officials had had enough and spoke up:

> Then Abishai son of Zeruiah said to the king, "Why should this dead dog curse my lord the king? Let me go over and cut off his head."
>
> 2 Samuel 16:9

Wouldn't you just love to have a trusted friend like Abishai? "Hey, David, if your ears are ringing and you're getting tired of getting pelted with rocks, I can solve the problem real fast. Just say the word and I'll head over there and give him a splitting headache. Come on, David. What do you say?" At the time, I'm sure this was a tempting offer for David. But verse 10 makes it clear that the "man after God's own heart" would have nothing to do with any retaliatory bloodshed:

> But the king said, "What do you and I have in common, you sons of Zeruiah? If he is cursing because the LORD said to him, 'Curse David,' who can ask, 'Why do you do this?'"
>
> 2 Samuel 16:10

David was a remarkable follower of God. There is so much maturity and wisdom in what he said here. What David heard from Shimei here in 2 Samuel 16 is not much different from what every one of us hears from *our own* critics. But how David handled this criticism and slander was remarkable.

You see, when an *immature* man is slandered by another, he will retaliate—trying to get the person to shut up by throwing plenty of slanderous jabs of his own. When a *mature* man is slandered by another, he will *not* retaliate with a tit-for-tat response. Instead, he will try to filter out the grains of truth in the criticism. Why? Because the mature man or woman realizes that, almost without exception, there is a grain of truth in every criticism. When a *godly* man is slandered by another, he will not only look at it as a learning experience but will consider the possibility that God is working through the slander.

Remember what the godly man Job said when he lost almost everything he valued.

> When a mature man is slandered by another, he will not retaliate with a tit-for-tat response. Instead, he will try to filter out the grains of truth in the criticism.

He fell to the ground in worship and said, "Naked I came from my mother's womb and naked I will depart. The LORD gave and the LORD has taken away; may the name of the LORD be praised."

Job 1:20-21

And then we read in the next verse:

In all this, Job did not sin by charging God with wrongdoing.

Job 1:22

In chapter 2, as Job's wife was trying to convince him to curse God and die, he responded with these wise words:

> "You are talking like a foolish woman. Shall we accept good from God and not trouble?"

> Job 2:10

The truth is: We are much better at receiving *compliments* than *criticism*. We can be quick to thank God when people encourage us, but we rarely thank Him when people criticize us. Think about it: Have you ever been cussed out and thanked the LORD for it? I doubt many of us have prayed, "Thank you, Jesus! I know that You're working through this cussing. I know that You're using this slander and these wretched comments to draw me closer to You. If it's part of Your plan, feel free to allow someone else to cuss me out tomorrow."

> I doubt many of us have prayed, "Thank you, Jesus! I know that You're at work. If it's part of Your plan, feel free to allow someone else to cuss me out tomorrow."

When it comes down to it, you and I have plenty of room for improvement. Sooner or later someone will cover us with verbal sewage. It's not a matter of *if* but *when*. So how will you handle it? How are you going to respond? You've got three options.

Option #1: Are you going to handle it with *immaturity*, tossing some verbal sewage right back at the person who verbally abuses you?

Option #2: Are you going to handle it with *simple maturity*, searching through the sewage for some grains of truth that you can learn from and grow? or

Option #3: Are you going to handle it with *godliness*, actually considering the possibility that God is working through the wretched person who is spilling all over you, and in turn respond with a "Thank you, Jesus"?

74

Following Jesus isn't easy, is it?

So David and his men continued along the road while Shimei was going along the hillside opposite him, cursing as he went and throwing stones at him and showering him with dirt. The king and all the people with him arrived at their destination exhausted. And there he refreshed himself.

2 Samuel 16:13-14

Shimei Does Some Back-Pedaling

Quite a bit happens in the next few chapters of 2 Samuel. Absalom was killed, and David returned to Jerusalem as the rightful king. And as David made his way back to Jerusalem, guess who ran to meet him and did some quick back-pedaling? You guessed it... good ol' Shimei.

> When Shimei son of Gera crossed the Jordan, he fell prostrate before the king and said to him, "May my lord not hold me guilty. Do not remember how your servant did wrong on the day my lord the king left Jerusalem. May the king put it out of his mind. For I your servant know that I have sinned, but today I have come here as the first of the whole house of Joseph to come down and meet my lord the king."

2 Samuel 19:18b-20

Shimei fell on his face before David, called him "lord" three different times and begged for mercy and forgiveness. So David extended it to him, speaking these words:

"Should anyone be put to death in Israel today? Do I not know that today I am king over Israel?" So the king said to Shimei, "You shall not die." And the king promised him on oath.

2 Samuel 19:22b-23

But some ten years later as David was on his deathbed giving instructions to his son Solomon, David told Solomon to deal with Shimei however he saw fit. (See 1 Kings 2:8-9.) Solomon chose to require Shimei to remain within Jerusalem so that he could keep a watchful eye on him. Solomon was practicing the old adage: "Keep your friends close and your enemies even closer."

Long story short: Shimei defied Solomon's order and was put to death as a punishment. (See 1 Kings 2:39-46.) It may have taken some twelve-to-fifteen years, but Shimei was punished for his reckless cursing and pummeling of God's chosen king.

3 Life Lessons

Consider these three life lessons from this passage: one lesson each from God, King David and Shimei.

Life Lesson #1: A Lesson from God: God doesn't waste anything. He can even use a screaming, cussing, dirt-throwing yahoo to fulfill His purposes and draw us closer to Him. Consider this: We will never believe that God is at work in *every* area of our lives until we believe that God is at work in the criticism. And we can never really give God the praise He deserves until we can praise Him not only *in the midst of* the criticism but also *for* the criticism.

Never forget the wise words of Job: "The LORD gave and the LORD has taken away; may the name of the LORD be praised." And Job's question to his wife is just as crucial to remember: "Shall we accept good from God and not trouble?" If you and I are serious about becoming mature in our faith and becoming more like Jesus, then we *have* to allow God to stretch us and humble us through criticism, even when it comes from rude, obnoxious, hateful individuals like Shimei.

Life Lesson #2: A Lesson from David: When undergoing criticism, our human tendency is to shoot the messenger, but a spiritually mature person disciplines himself/herself to search for the grain of truth. Believe me, over the years of my life, I've been called just about every foul name in the book. But I have become convinced that there is a grain of truth in every criticism. So even when I'm on the receiving end of some of the worst profanity-strewn verbal barrages, I try hard to search for the grains of truth. And

> If we are serious about becoming mature in our faith, then we have to allow God to stretch us and humble us through criticism, even when it comes from rude, obnoxious, hateful individuals like Shimei.

in doing so, I have grown tremendously. Had I shot the messenger, no growth would have taken place. It would have been my loss.

The same holds true for you. It isn't always easy. When the verbal sewage is flowing, it may sting quite a bit, and the grain of truth may not be apparent to you at the time. But if you ask the LORD humbly, "What do you want me to learn from this?" I believe He will reveal the lesson(s) to you in time.

Just like me, you have had Shimeis in your life and will most likely have new Shimeis around you in the years to come. It's not a question of *if* but *when*. So how are you going to respond to your Shimeis? When you are being pelted with four-letter words and slander and dirt, will you retaliate in kind, or will you handle it with maturity and godliness? Will you fight fire with fire—stunting your opportunity for growth—or will you look for the grains of truth in the criticism and praise God for what He's teaching you?

Life Lesson #3: A Lesson from Shimei: Just because God may use your wretched behavior for His purposes doesn't mean He condones it. "Be sure that your sin will find you out." (See Numbers 32:23.) After twenty years, Shimei's sin found him out. He reaped what he had sown.

It's a principle that we see repeated time and time again in Scripture. Jonah sowed seeds of disobedience and reaped a mouthful of whale blubber and seaweed. David sowed seeds of adultery and reaped a family disaster. Israel sowed seeds of complaining and rebellion and reaped death in the desert. So remember: Just because God may use a person's wretched behavior for His purposes, it doesn't mean He condones it. A person will reap what he sows. Be sure your sins will find you out.

A Final Question

One final question: Are you someone else's Shimei? Have you been spewing verbal sewage over someone you know? Have you been speaking discouragement, disrespect and hatred into another's life? Every one of us can be "nicey nice" on a Sunday morning at church, but how are you treating your spouse behind closed doors? How are you treating your kids? How are you treating your parents? A Christian should never be a Shimei. And if you are, be warned: You will reap what you sow, and it won't be pretty. Just ask Shimei.

CHAPTER 7

Micaiah Son of Imlah

He Stood for Truth in a Crowd of Liars

Have you ever been duped by someone's exaggerated or deceitful sales pitch? "You need to buy this exercise machine. In just five minutes a day you can burn fat, build muscle and sculpt your abs! You'll look like Mr. Universe or a supermodel in just thirty days." You bought the slick sales pitch hook, line and sinker, and now your too-good-to-be-true exercise machine is gathering dust in the corner of the garage. As soon as you have your next yard sale, it will be loaded into the vehicle of some other sucker who saw the infomercial but will get to take it home for a lot less money.

Does it sound like I'm speaking from personal experience? That's because...I am. Early in my marriage my wife and I unloaded several hundred dollars on a "state-of-the-art" exercise machine. I won't mention the brand, but it was one of those newfangled elliptical trainers. Boy, did we have high hopes of getting toned and fit, but after a few short months of owning the machine, we were *not* in much better shape, and the machine was starting to make funny noises. Oops! Lesson learned.

Maybe you haven't fallen prey to a slick infomercial sales pitch, but you've been duped in other ways. Maybe you've had a friend come to you and say, "I have the perfect guy/girl for you. You two would be *so* perfect for each other!" So how'd that work out for you? Perhaps a family member or coworker persuaded you to "invest" your hard-earned money in their latest get-rich-quick scheme (i.e., a pile of lottery tickets). You didn't strike it rich, did you? Or possibly the bank has courted you and said, "Sure you can afford this $3,000-a-month mortgage. In fact, we'll even let you cash out up to $50,000." It sounded too good to be true—and it was.

Oh, there's no shortage of crummy advice, slick sales pitches and flat-out lies coming our way, is there? No one likes to be duped. None of us wants to be sold a bill of goods. Thankfully, God's word has much to teach us about *discerning* and *speaking* the truth. I imagine

> I imagine that you, like me, want to get better at distinguishing between godly advice and shoddy advice.

that you, like me, want to get better at distinguishing between *godly* advice and *shoddy* advice. As we turn to 1 Kings 22, we'll be learning some valuable lessons about discerning the truth and standing up for truth even when we find ourselves surrounded by liars.

The Nation Divides and Rebels

King Solomon was a good and godly king in his early years, but as he got older, his Achilles' heel became very clear: beautiful, exotic women who didn't follow God. By the end of his life, Solomon had married a staggering 700 different women and had amassed another 300 concubines. And because Solomon was a sucker for a pretty face, these foreign women led him astray. They persuaded him to worship idols, and as a result, Solomon's devotion to God was only half-hearted. (Solomon's downfall is explained in 1 Kings 11:1-13.)

In response to Solomon's *divided* loyalties, the LORD divided Israel in two: ten tribes in the North and two tribes in the South. For the sake of David, God gave Solomon's sons and grandsons the two southern tribes to lead, but God handed the ten northern tribes over to another leader. (In the Old Testament the ten northern tribes are called Israel, Samaria or Ephraim, and the two southern tribes are called Judah.)

Sadly, as the years went by, Israel strayed further and further from the LORD while Judah's faithfulness to the LORD was hit-and-miss. The events of 1 Kings 22 took place about eighty years after the kingdom had divided into two nations. During this eighty-year period, Israel had already had seven different kings, and not a single one followed the LORD.

The first king of Israel was Jeroboam. He set up two golden calves in the city of Bethel, and he told the people that those two calves were the gods who had led them out of Egypt. Jeroboam also built pagan worship centers on the hillsides and selected men to be priests who weren't qualified. Jeroboam was a real piece of work, but he seemed like Mother Teresa compared to the seventh king of Israel, King Ahab.

You may remember Ahab as the king who was married to one of the most wicked women in the Bible: Jezebel. The writer of the Book of Kings describes him this way:

> In the thirty-eighth year of Asa king of Judah, Ahab son of Omri became king of Israel, and he reigned in Samaria over Israel twenty-two years. Ahab son of Omri did more evil in the eyes of the LORD than any of those before him. He not only considered it trivial to commit the sins of Jeroboam son of Nebat, but he also married Jezebel daughter of Ethbaal king of the Sidonians, and began to serve Baal and worship him. He set up an altar for Baal in the temple of Baal that he built in Samaria. Ahab also made an Asherah pole and did more to provoke the LORD,

the God of Israel, to anger than did all the kings of Israel before him.

1 Kings 16:29-33

Here's a quick description of the main characters in 1 Kings 22:

King Ahab (pronounced, "**AY-hab**") = the evil king of Israel (the Northern Kingdom).

King Jehoshaphat (pronounced, "**ji-HOSH-uh-fat**") = the good king of Judah (the Southern Kingdom) who followed the LORD faithfully but formed unwise alliances with evil kings.

Micaiah son of Imlah (pronounced, "**mi-KAY-yuh**") = a true prophet of the LORD who spoke God's truth regardless of whether or not people around him wanted to hear it.

An Unwise Alliance

At this point in history, one of the most troublesome enemies of Israel was the nation of Aram, sometimes called Syria. Back in chapter 20, King Ahab led Israel in battle against King Ben-Hadad, king of Aram, and King Ahab's army cleaned Ben-Hadad's clock. The Aramean king ended up surrendering, and as part of his surrender, he promised to return all the cities to King Ahab that the prior king had besieged. To King Ahab this was fantastic news, but there was one small problem: Ben-Hadad lied. Here in chapter 22, Ben-Hadad had yet to return the city of Ramoth Gilead to Israel. Beginning in verse 2, the scene is set.

Jehoshaphat king of Judah went down to see the king of Israel.

> 1 Kings 22:2

Now, King Jehoshaphat was a good and godly king. The writer of 1 Kings makes this clear later in the chapter:

> In everything [Jehoshaphat] walked in the ways of his father Asa and did not stray from them; he did what was right in the eyes of the LORD.
>
> 1 Kings 22:43

However, like Solomon before him, King Jehoshaphat had an Achilles' heel. Unlike Solomon, his greatest weakness wasn't foreign women. It was his tendency to make treaties with wicked, foreign kings. He got himself into trouble with God on several occasions during his reign, because he just didn't understand this simple truth: If you lie down with dogs, you will wake up with fleas. The Apostle Paul said it this way in his first letter to the Corinthians:

> Bad company corrupts good character.
>
> 1 Corinthians 15:33

Here in 1 Kings 22, King Jehoshaphat foolishly aligned himself with Ahab, the wicked king of Israel.

> The king of Israel had said to his officials, "Don't you know that Ramoth Gilead belongs to us and yet we are doing nothing to retake it from the king of Aram?" So he asked Jehoshaphat, "Will you go with me to fight against Ramoth Gilead?" Jehoshaphat replied to the king of Israel,

"I am as you are, my people as your people, my horses as your horses."

1 Kings 22:3-4

Oh no! Jehoshaphat, what are you doing? I hope you don't really mean what you're saying. Ahab wasn't just a *bad* king; he was the *most wicked* king that Israel had ever had! He and his wife were both murderers. He was a selfish, greedy thief who rejected the LORD and worshiped idols of wood and stone instead. And he and his wife tried their best to kill all of the LORD's true prophets so that the Israelites couldn't worship God even if they had wanted to. Making an alliance with King Ahab was like making an alliance with Osama bin Laden. It was madness! But nonetheless, that's what Jehoshaphat did.

> "Bad company corrupts good character."
> 1 Corinthians 15:33

The Parade of Prophets

Fortunately, Jehoshaphat did have one requirement of Ahab before he committed his own troops to battle. In verse 5 Jehoshaphat asked Ahab to "First seek the counsel of the LORD." Although Jehoshaphat had spoken too soon about being united with King Ahab, at least he was insistent about finding out what God thought about it.

So King Ahab brought together four hundred prophets to consult. Sounds good, doesn't it? Sadly however, these were *bogus* prophets. In all likelihood, these were prophets-for-hire hand-picked by King Ahab to oversee the worship of the golden calves. And he was so proud of them. They *looked* good, and they made him *feel* so good. After all, they had a habit of telling King Ahab exactly what his itching ears wanted to hear. This being the case, these were not prophets that God had ordained to an *authentic* ministry but prophets that a wicked king had ordained to a *counterfeit* ministry.

Once the four hundred prophets made their grand entrance into the courtyard, King Ahab asked them the question of the hour: "Shall I go to war against Ramoth Gilead, or shall I refrain?" (verse 6). And how do you suppose these bogus prophets on the king's payroll responded? According to verse 6, they all responded in unison, "Go, for the LORD will give it into the king's hand."

That settles it...right? There was a 100% consensus among these prophets. You can't get more unanimous than 100%. This battle was going to be a slam-dunk, right?

Well, not so fast! King Jehoshaphat smelled something fishy. There was something that wasn't quite right about these prophets. They probably *looked* like prophets of the LORD and *dressed* like prophets of the LORD and *spoke* like prophets of the LORD. But Jehoshaphat knew that these four hundred yahoos were *not* prophets of the LORD.

In verse 7 Jehoshaphat turned to Ahab and asked: "Is there not a prophet of the LORD here whom we can inquire of?" You've got to just *love* Jehoshaphat. He had discerned the charade for what it was. In essence, he told King Ahab, "These prophets of yours aren't any good. They're pretend prophets. Where is the *real* prophet who is *really* going to speak the word of the LORD?"

We would expect King Ahab to have been offended by Jehoshaphat's question...and he was! Verse 8 makes it clear that Jehoshaphat's question really chapped Ahab's hide.

> The King of Israel answered Jehoshaphat, "There is still one man through whom we can inquire of the LORD, but I hate him because he never prophesies anything good about me, but always bad. He is Micaiah son of Imlah."
>
> 1 Kings 22:8

This response of Ahab was a red flag waving in Jehoshaphat's face, a red flag that should have caused him to turn and run. Ahab wasn't interested in hearing godly advisers who spoke the truth, but only in hearing "yes" men who spoke a feel-good message. Jehoshaphat must have had spiritual sirens going off in his mind blaring: "Abort! Abort! Abort! Get yourself as far away from this evil king as you possibly can!" But instead of pulling the plug on his ill-conceived alliance and hitting the road, Jehoshaphat stayed put. He simply gave Ahab a slap on the wrist, saying, "The king should not say that" (verse 8).

In verses 9-14 the drama builds. King Ahab ordered his servants to summon Micaiah as he and King Jehoshaphat sat side-by-side on their thrones near the city gate. The two kings were decked out in their royal robes, and the four hundred false prophets were dancing around them, whooping and hollering their whale-of-a-tale prophecies.

This scene was so contrived, and it became even more contrived as one of the prophets named Zedekiah son of Kenaanah stepped forward. He had made himself some little iron horns. (He was probably holding up two iron spikes on the side of his head. *Idiot!*) And in verse 11 he boldly proclaimed to the two kings sitting in front of him: "This is what the LORD says: 'With these you will gore the Arameans until they are destroyed.'"

The other prophets were eating it up. They just loved the little spiky-horn illustration, and they cackled in unison, "Attack Ramoth Gilead and be victorious, for the LORD will give it into the king's hand" (verse 12). The scene that had unfolded in front of them seemed flawless to King Ahab, a Tony-Award-winning production worthy of an encore. But that all changed in one moment.

In Walked Micaiah

The messenger King Ahab had sent to get Micaiah had given him a strong-armed word of advice as he brought him before the kings: "Look, as one man the other prophets are predicting success for the king. Let your word agree with theirs, and speak favorably" (verse 13). Wasn't that helpful advice? "Micaiah, don't do what you normally do. Don't stir the pot. Don't rock the boat. Just tell the king what he wants to hear." But we quickly discover that Micaiah wasn't about to play the king's game. He responded to the messenger: "As surely as the LORD lives, I can tell him only what the LORD tells me" (verse 14).

> Everyone needs a friend who is bold enough to say, "I'm not going to tell you what your itching ears *want* to hear. I'm going to tell you what you *need* to hear."

Oh, every one of us needs a friend like Micaiah! Everyone needs a friend who is bold enough to get in his/her face and say, "I don't care what everybody else has told you, I'm going to tell you the truth. I'm going to point you to what God's word says without watering it down. I'm not going to tell you what your itching ears *want* to hear. I'm going to tell you what you *need* to hear." Oh, don't we all need a friend who speaks the truth in love?

In verse 15 Micaiah arrived, and King Ahab asked him the same question that he had asked his own four hundred prophets: "Micaiah, shall we go to war against Ramoth Gilead, or shall I refrain?"

You could have heard a pin drop. Two kings, their officials and four hundred prophets were listening intently to Micaiah's response, which was, "Attack and be victorious... for the LORD will give it into the king's hand."

You'd think that King Ahab would be delighted to hear Micaiah speak these words, but it's clear that he wasn't. Micaiah's tone of voice must have been dripping with sarcasm, because King Ahab snapped back at him, "How many times must I make you swear to tell me nothing but the truth in the name of the LORD?" (verse 16). So in response to Ahab's question, Micaiah shared the honest truth:

> Then Micaiah answered, "I saw all Israel scattered on the hills like sheep without a shepherd, and the LORD said, 'These people have no master. Let each one go home in peace.'"

> 1 Kings 22:17

Translation: The Army of Israel would be defeated on the battlefield. King Ahab would be killed, and the surviving soldiers would have no choice but to retreat and go back home.

There it was—the honest truth that no other prophet in the courtyard had been brave enough (or discerning enough) to speak. King Ahab should have been grateful for Micaiah's honesty. After all, heeding Micaiah's counsel would save Ahab a world of hurt. Heeding his counsel would be life-saving—literally. But Ahab didn't express an inkling of gratitude. Instead, he turned to Jehoshaphat in verse 18 and said, "Didn't I tell you that he never prophesies anything good about me, but only bad?"

Well, much to King Ahab's chagrin, Micaiah wasn't finished talking. Micaiah painted a more detailed picture of the events that had unfolded. He explained how God had permitted a lying spirit to speak through the four hundred false prophets with the express purpose of enticing Ahab to go to his death on the battlefield. And do you remember Zedekiah…the guy with the little iron horns? He didn't like Micaiah accusing him of having a lying spirit in his mouth. He didn't like it one bit, so he walked up to Micaiah and slapped him in the face, saying, "Which way did the spirit from the LORD go when he went from me to speak to you?" (verse 24).

King Ahab had heard enough of Micaiah's prophesying, so he gave the order to put Micaiah in prison with only the most basic of rations: bread and water. But as Micaiah was being escorted out of the courtyard, he interjected one final word of warning.

> Micaiah declared, "If you ever return safely, the LORD has not spoken through me." Then he added, "Mark my words, all you people!"
>
> 1 Kings 22:28

I just love Micaiah! He's one of my favorite little-known heroes. Even as he was being unfairly criticized, abused and imprisoned, he maintained his bold stance for the truth. And within a few short days, everyone in the courtyard realized the truth. Despite Micaiah's warnings, King Ahab and King Jehoshaphat went to battle against the army of Aram, and they paid a high price. Just as Micaiah had prophesied, the armies of Israel and Judah were soundly defeated. King Jehoshaphat barely escaped with his life, and King Ahab was killed on the battlefield.

4 Life Lessons

Life Lesson #1: A Lesson from King Jehoshaphat: It is foolish to make alliances with wicked men. Paul reminds us of this truth in his second letter to the Corinthians.

> Do not be yoked together with unbelievers. For what do righteousness and wickedness have in common? Or what fellowship can light have with darkness? What harmony is there between Christ and [the devil]? What does a believer have in common with an unbeliever?
>
> 2 Corinthians 6:14-15

This is a crucial principle for Christian living: "Do not be yoked together with unbelievers." This principle applies to marriage: Christians should *not* marry non-Christians. (And that being the case, it is unwise for Christians to be *engaged to* or even *date* non-Christians.) When a man and woman are in a committed relationship but aren't on the same page spiritually, it's playing with fire. Too often hearts are broken and relationships are strained when couples don't hold the same values and beliefs.

I would also suggest that this principle applies to counseling relationships. If you are a Christian and need professional counseling, you're taking an unnecessary risk by seeking counsel from a therapist who doesn't share your Christian values and beliefs. Whenever possible, a Christian should choose a Christian counselor.

And this great biblical principle even applies to our business partnerships. We need to seek partnerships with Christian business associates. Any close relationship—personal, clinical or professional—should be "equally yoked" whenever possible. Jehoshaphat's foolhardy alliance with Ahab and refusal to heed Micaiah's counsel led to disastrous results on the battlefield. Jehoshaphat ignored the truth that Micaiah had spoken, and he suffered the consequences. He learned the hard way that it is foolish to make alliances with wicked men.

> Any close relationship—personal, clinical or professional—should be "equally yoked" whenever possible.

Life Lesson #2: A Lesson from King Ahab: Each of us has to decide—Will I surround myself with "yes men" who tell me what *I* want to hear or with God-fearing men/women who tell me what *God* wants me to hear? Ahab made his decision. He opted for the "yes men." But what is your decision? God's word to us is so timely in Paul's second letter to Timothy:

For the time will come when men will not put up with sound doctrine. Instead, to suit their own desires, they will gather around them a great number of teachers to say what their itching ears want to hear. They will turn their ears away from the truth and turn aside to myths.

2 Timothy 4:3-4

Friend, if you are serious about becoming more like Jesus, then you don't need advice-givers around you who stroke your ego and pamper your feelings. If you are serious about becoming more like Jesus, there's no way around it: You *need* godly friends and advisors who speak the truth to you, even when it hurts. You must seek friends and advisors who are more concerned with pleasing *God* than they are with pleasing *you.* Got it? On any given day, the godly counsel of one honest person is more valuable than the counsel of four hundred "yes" men.

Life Lesson 3: A Lesson from Zedekiah Son of Kenaanah: Speaking lies in the name of the LORD brings swift judgment. So be very cautious when saying, "This is the word of the LORD." Do you know what the biblical test of a true prophet is? We find it in Deuteronomy 18:15-22. According to this great passage of Scripture, the biblical requirement for every prophet of the LORD is 100% accuracy, 100% of the time.

> According to Deuteronomy 18:15-22, the requirement for every prophet of the LORD is 100% accuracy, 100% of the time.

In Old Testament times if a prophet in Israel spoke presumptuously in the name of the LORD even once, that prophet was put to death. So I have a question for you. In Old Testament times, what would you call a prophet who spoke accurately in the name of the LORD 99.9% of the time? The answer: You would call him…a *dead* prophet. Under God's standards, a prophet could not speak God's word inaccurately even once and live to tell about it.

With this in mind, we have to be *very* careful whenever we say, "God told me to tell you such and such" or "It is God's will that you do this or that." We had better make sure that if we speak in the name of the LORD, what we are saying is backed up by Scripture. Zedekiah and his other three hundred ninety-nine buddies failed the biblical test of a true prophet. Despite their bold predictions, Ahab's army was defeated on the battlefield. Ahab himself was killed, and we can be sure that God brought swift punishment on these false prophets for speaking lies in His name.

Life Lesson #4: A Lesson from Micaiah: Boldly stand for truth and speak God's word even when nobody else will. If you are living with

> In this day and age when many Christians would rather stretch the truth to avoid "stirring the pot," don't be afraid to do a little stirring.

a spouse who refuses to stand for the truth of God's word, stand for God's truth anyway. If you are in a circle of friends where all the people in the group are tickling each others' itching ears with lies and half-truths that they *want* to hear, be the *true* friend who speaks the truth that they *need* to hear. If you are in a work environment where lying and cheating are the norm, be different: Speak the truth and work with integrity. If you are in a school where God is mocked and the Bible is discarded, boldly stand for God's word in your school anyway.

And by all means, if you ever have the opportunity to produce an infomercial, don't embellish, and don't exaggerate. Please tell your audience the truth.

In this day and age when many Christians would rather stretch the truth to avoid "stirring the pot," don't be afraid to do a little stirring. Even if four hundred so-called "experts" are standing in unison and saying what everybody *wants* to hear, you need to stand and speak what everybody *needs* to hear: the truth—God's truth—revealed in His word, the Bible. Be like Micaiah! When you find yourself in a crowd of liars, stand for truth.

CHAPTER 8

Gehazi

He Threw It All Away for a Moment's Pleasure

A while back I was in my office at church preparing a sermon. With my right hand I reached for a reference book on the shelf as I placed my left hand on the arm of my couch. But to my surprise, I felt something strange underneath my left hand, something that was out of place. After moving my hand I was shocked to discover a few little brown pellets lying there on the arm of my couch—mouse pellets. The evidence was conclusive: There was a mouse in my office, and one of us *had* to go!

After thoroughly washing my hand, I placed baited mouse traps in strategic locations around the church building. And within twenty-four hours *I got him!* Fievel the Mouse had met his Maker! All it took was a little bit of peanut butter on the platform of the mouse trap, and *wham!* Bye-bye, mouse.

As I picked up the sprung trap and transported the flat-headed little fellow to the dumpster, I wanted to ask him: "Was it worth it? You had just begun to touch the peanut butter with your little, mousy tongue. Your taste buds had just barely begun to register the salty flavor of the peanut butter in your mouth when the trap sprung. So was it worth it?" And I could almost hear the little mouse answer back: "*Squeak squeak, squeak squeak.*" For those of you who don't speak mouse, it translates: "Not on your life!"

Friends, the mouse trap is a perfect illustration of the trappings of sin. You see, every sin is the sacrificing of God's long-term blessings for brief, momentary pleasure. Whether it's sexual sin, an addiction, lying, cheating, stealing, gossip or cursing—whatever the sin may be—it is the forfeiting of God's enduring rewards for a short, cheap thrill.

In recent years thousands of lives have been cut short as the result of drunk driving. What massive devastation has resulted from a few moments of drinking pleasure! Thousands

> Sin is the sacrificing of God's long-term blessings for brief, momentary pleasure.

of marriages have been devastated because of pornography and affairs. How many families have been torn apart in exchange for a few moments of sexual pleasure? And countless churches have been permanently wounded because of gossip and slander. God alone knows how much the unity and effectiveness of churches have been compromised by Christians who have chosen the temporary pleasure of passing on the latest dirt instead of just cleaning it up. So much hurt, so much heartache, so much devastation…all for a moment's pleasure.

As we turn to the book of 2 Kings, we'll learn some valuable life lessons from a man named Gehazi (pronounced, "**gi-HAY-zee**"), who squandered one of life's greatest privileges for a few bucks. Most of the little-known men and women we've been learning about so far are heroes, followers of God who we *want* to emulate. Gehazi is *not* one of them. I hope and pray that you and I will not make the same foolish mistakes that Gehazi made in 2 Kings 5.

Gehazi: A Model Servant

The setting was northern Israel. It had been around one hundred forty years since David had been king, about one hundred years since Israel was split in two. Sadly, during the two hundred years that northern Israel ("Samaria") existed as a separate nation, every one of her kings was evil. Every one worshiped idols. Every one turned his back on God. Every one ignored God's laws.

So as we read through 1 and 2 Kings, we come across plenty of *discouragement*. The LORD's chosen people were almost indistinguishable from the pagan nations around them. After all that God had done for the Israelites—delivering them out of Egypt, providing food and water for them in the desert, blessing them with the Promised Land and rescuing them from their enemies—the Israelites *still* turned their backs on the LORD.

But in the midst of reading discouraging report after discouraging report, there are two breaths of fresh air in northern Israel—two powerful prophets God raised up to perform miracles and point Israel back to God. Their names were Elijah and Elisha.

In 2 Kings 5, Elisha was in the early part of his ministry. Elijah had already been taken up to Heaven in a whirlwind, and Elisha was continuing Elijah's ministry in a powerful way. Elisha's ministry was *so* powerful, in fact, that he ended up becoming one of the greatest miracle workers in the entire Old Testament, second only to Moses. Not until Jesus' ministry some eight hundred years later would anyone perform as many miracles as Elisha.

In 2 Kings 4, Elisha had performed his greatest miracle: raising a young boy from the dead. It's in the same chapter that we are introduced to Gehazi. His name first appears in verse 12 where he is simply referred to as Elisha's "servant." It seems clear that Gehazi was the chief assistant who served Elisha in much the same way that Elisha had served Elijah in the months leading up to his fiery departure to heaven. (See 2 Kings 2:11-12.)

Gehazi was a pretty busy fellow throughout chapter 4, and it appears he was a faithful and obedient servant. As we read though the chapter (particularly verses 11-37), Elisha barked out orders to Gehazi, and Gehazi obeyed every one. Every parent would love his/her kids to obey as quickly and completely as Gehazi obeyed Elisha in chapter 4.

Wouldn't you agree that one of the biggest frustrations parents face is trying to get our kids to listen and obey Mommy and Daddy's orders *the first time*? Our kids obey us...*eventually*. But that's not true obedience, is it? In chapter 4, Gehazi did a marvelous job of obeying his master quickly without arguing, complaining or procrastinating. Unfortunately, in chapter 5 Gehazi got bit by "the stupid bug," and as a result found himself in a load of trouble with both Elisha and God.

A Foreigner Is Miraculously Healed

In chapter 5 we are introduced to a soldier named Naaman (pronounced, **"NAY-uh-muhn"**), who is described this way in verse 1:

> Now Naaman was commander of the army of the king of Aram. He was a great man in the sight of his master and highly regarded, because through him the LORD had given victory to Aram. He was a valiant soldier, but he had leprosy.
>
> 2 Kings 5:1

During this period, Israel and Aram were neighbors who struggled with an on-again-off-again relationship. Although the events of chapter 5 likely took place during a period of peace between these two nations, it had only been a few short years since the two neighbors had been at war. In fact, it was the army of Aram that had killed King Ahab on the battlefield in 1 Kings 22.

Among other things, this chapter reinforces the biblical truth that God cares about people of all nations, not just the people of Israel. Because of this reality, churches today send missionaries to the most remote tribes in Kenya, Myanmar and Peru. We do so because God is concerned about the souls of every last person in every last tribe on earth. This includes army commanders in ancient Aram.

It's clear from 2 Kings 5:1 that the LORD's hand of blessing was upon Naaman. As Naaman led Aram's army in its military campaigns, God brought him victory after victory. Why would God do that? Evidently, God did so because it was part of His plan, a plan that involved Naaman's healing. Verse 1 ends with these words: "He was a valiant soldier, but he had leprosy."

The word "leprosy" as used in the Bible is a general word that included a variety of skin diseases. As leprosy is described in the Old Testament, it seems to have been something like psoriasis or eczema. It was ugly; it was irritating; at times it may have even smelled, and some forms of it may have been contagious. Naaman had a form of leprosy, and he was sick of it. He would have done just about anything to get rid of it.

> God cares about people of all nations, not just the people of Israel. God is concerned about the souls of every last person on earth.

As the chapter unfolds, things get pretty interesting. In verse 2 we discover that Naaman's wife had a servant girl who was an Israelite, and like most other Israelites, she knew *all about* Elisha. After all, the miracle-working prophet was quickly becoming a living legend in Israel. The little girl boldly spoke up in verse 3:

"If only my master would see the prophet who is in Samaria! He would cure him of his leprosy."

2 Kings 5:3

Well, long story short: Naaman thought that going to see Israel's legendary prophet was a *great* idea. So within a short time, he and his traveling companions were standing on Elisha's front doorstep. In verse 10 Elisha sent a messenger (likely Gehazi) to the door with these instructions for Naaman:

"Go, wash yourself seven times in the Jordan, and your flesh will be restored and you will be cleansed."

2 Kings 5:10

After throwing a small temper tantrum and refusing to carry out Elisha's odd instructions, Naaman relented and obeyed. And according to verse 14, the results were dramatic:

So he went down and dipped himself in the Jordan seven times, as the man of God had told him, and his flesh was restored and became clean like that of a young boy.

2 Kings 5:14

As you can imagine, Naaman was thrilled! He was so excited that he returned to Elisha's house and enthusiastically shared the good news:

"Now I know that there is no God in all the world except in Israel. Please accept now a gift from your servant."

2 Kings 5:15

God's power working through Elisha was so evident that Naaman committed himself to God on the spot. And he was so appreciative, so thankful, that he insisted on giving Elisha a generous gift before leaving. But Elisha refused to accept it.

> "As surely as the LORD lives, whom I serve, I will not accept a thing." And even though Naaman urged him, he refused.
>
> 2 Kings 5:16

From Elisha's perspective, God's miracles were always to be offered free of charge. Acts of compassion and mercy were never to be done for compensation and personal gain but for the good of others and God's glory.

> **Acts of compassion and mercy are never to be done for compensation and personal gain but for the good of others and God's glory.**

In verse 19, Naaman left with his little caravan to go back home to Aram, but before leaving he promised Elisha that he would not make sacrifices to any other God but the LORD. In other words, Naaman committed to *follow* the LORD. This sounds like a very happy ending, doesn't it? It was. Unfortunately, Gehazi didn't agree.

Gehazi: A Model Servant No Longer

Maybe it was resentment. Perhaps it was greed. Whatever it was, Gehazi stepped onto the scene and made a mockery of a beautiful, selfless miracle.

> Gehazi, the servant of Elisha the man of God, said to himself, "My master was too easy on Naaman, this Aramean, by not accepting from him what he brought. As surely as the LORD lives, I will run after him and get something from him." So Gehazi hurried after Naaman.

When Naaman saw him running toward him, he got down from the chariot to meet him. "Is everything all right?" he asked. "Everything is all right," Gehazi answered. "My master sent me to say, 'Two young men from the company of the prophets have just come to me from the hill country of Ephraim. Please give them a talent of silver and two sets of clothing.'" "By all means, take two talents," said Naaman. He urged Gehazi to accept them, and then tied up the two talents of silver in two bags, with two sets of clothing. He gave them to two of his servants, and they carried them ahead of Gehazi. When Gehazi came to the hill, he took the things from the servants and put them away in the house. He sent the men away and they left.

2 Kings 5:20-24

Notice the self-centered greed in Gehazi's words: "*I* will get something from him." Gehazi wasn't concerned about *Elisha*. He wasn't concerned about *Naaman*, and he certainly wasn't concerned about *God*. So Gehazi ran like a madman to catch up with Naaman, and when he caught up to him, he lied like a rug. Gehazi concocted a fanciful story about two young prophets who had come to visit and needed some clothes and silver.

Naaman may or may not have believed Gehazi's story. But true story or not, he was delighted to comply with Gehazi's request. So he gave him the two sets of clothing and two pieces of silver instead of one. Naaman even sent two of his servants with Gehazi to help carry the clothes, but as they approached Elisha's house, Gehazi made sure to keep the servants out of sight. Gehazi hid the clothes and silver in the house and then presented himself to Elisha.

Gehazi should have known Elisha well enough to know that he was not easily fooled. The LORD's Spirit rested on Elisha in a powerful way. The same Spirit that enabled Elisha to perform great miracles could certainly enable him to see through his servant's deception.

> Then [Gehazi] went in and stood before his master Elisha. "Where have you been, Gehazi?" Elisha asked. "Your servant didn't go anywhere," Gehazi answered. But Elisha said to him, "Was not my spirit with you when the man got down from his chariot to meet you? Is this the time to take money, or to accept clothes, olive groves, vineyards, flocks, herds, or menservants and maidservants? Naaman's leprosy will cling to you and to your descendents forever." Then Gehazi went from Elisha's presence and he was leprous, as white as snow.
>
> 2 Kings 5:25-27

When Elisha asked Gehazi, "Where have you been?" he already knew the answer. Elisha, however, was giving Gehazi a chance to 'fess up and tell the truth. Instead, Gehazi chose to lie and continue his cover-up. That was a bad choice! He sealed his own fate. As a punishment, Gehazi was struck with Naaman's leprosy, and we read in verse 27 that Gehazi "went from Elisha's presence." This seems to mean that Gehazi was fired. He had forfeited the greatest privilege of his lifetime.

Never again do we read of Gehazi being in Elisha's service. In fact, he is only mentioned one more time in Scripture, in 2 Kings 8, where he brags to the King of Israel about Elisha's past miracles. Gehazi shares some wonderful stories of the good ol' days, but it's clear that Elisha is not with him. Gehazi had enjoyed one of the greatest privileges of his generation: to be the chief servant of one of the greatest miracle workers of the Old Testament. But he blew it. And as a result, his ministry years with Elisha came to a crashing halt.

4 Life Lessons

As I reflect on the bittersweet account of Gehazi's ministry in 2 Kings 4-5, I see several life lessons that we can draw from it. I offer you four lessons from Gehazi.

Life Lesson #1: Obey quickly and completely. When we take a careful look at the interactions between Elisha and Gehazi in chapter 4, we read of a model servant whose obedience was both quick and thorough. On two different occasions (in verses 12 & 15) Elisha asked Gehazi to call a certain widow into his presence, and Gehazi obeyed quickly and completely. In verses 25-26 Elisha commanded Gehazi to run to the widow and ask if she was "all right." Once again Gehazi obeyed quickly and completely. Similarly, in verses 29-31 Elisha commanded Gehazi to run speedily to the woman's house and lay his staff on her dead son's face. Yet again, Gehazi obeyed Elisha's instructions quickly and completely. There's no doubt that in chapter 4, Gehazi was quick to obey and follow instructions. He set a great example for us.

The Bible has much to say about how God responds to obedience and disobedience, and His response boils down to this: God pours out His mercy and blessing on those who obey His commands, but He pours out His judgment and wrath on those who rebel against His commands. God's message through the prophet Samuel to King Saul was this:

> "Does the LORD delight in burnt offerings and sacrifices as much as in obeying the voice of the LORD? To obey is better than sacrifice, and to heed is better than the fat of rams. For rebellion is like the sin of divination, and arrogance like the evil of idolatry."
>
> 1 Samuel 15:22-23a

Jesus made the same point to his disciples:

"If anyone loves me, he will obey my teaching."

John 14:23

In Ephesians 6:1 *children* are commanded to obey their parents. In Ephesians 6:5 *servants* (employees) are commanded to obey their earthly masters (bosses) with respect. In Hebrews 13:17 we are *all* commanded to obey our leaders, which includes both *government* leaders and our *church* leaders.

Therefore, any Christian who does *not* obey his/her leaders quickly and completely is living outside the will of God. In fact, according to that hard-hitting verse in 1 Samuel, disobedience or even *delayed obedience* are closer to witchcraft than they are to Christianity. *Ouch!* Chances are, you are a bigger rebel than you realize. We tend to be stubborn. We tend to push back at those in authority over us. We tend to be downright rebellious at times. And we need to stop it. We need to be like Gehazi in chapter 4: quick to listen and obey.

Life Lesson #2: Harboring resentment sets us on a path of destruction. When I was first jotting down lessons to learn from Gehazi, I wrote down 1 Timothy 6:10.

For the love of money is a root of all kinds of evil.

1 Timothy 6:10

Now, there's no doubt that this is a very important, biblical teaching. Loving money gets people into trouble. But the more I think about Gehazi, the more I think that his problem wasn't *greed* as much as it was *resentment*.

Take another look at 2 Kings 5:20 and see if you agree with me. Gehazi said to himself, "My master was too easy on Naaman, this Aramean, by not accepting from him what he brought." I can't help but wonder: Would Gehazi have done what he did here (lie, cheat and steal) if Naaman had been an *Israelite* army commander? I'm confident that the answer would be, "No."

It seems clear that Gehazi was prejudiced against Naaman because he was Aramean. Gehazi didn't like Arameans. They had, at times, been Israel's enemy, and he resented the fact that the Aramean army commander had come gallivanting to Elisha's house expecting a healing. And Elisha was letting him get away with it. "Well," thought Gehazi, "Not if I can help it."

> Harboring resentment sets us on a path of destruction. So let it go.

Let me ask you, are you carrying a burden similar to Gehazi's: a burden of resentment? Possibly you're filled with resentment against your *parents* for how they raised you. Maybe you're harboring resentment against your *ex-husband* or *ex-wife* who broke your heart or against your *boss* who fired you. Perhaps it's directed at a *teacher* who failed you or a *drunk driver* whose reckless behavior stole a loved one away from you. You resent the fact that that person has *said* what he's said and *done* what he's done. Let me just say this simply and clearly: *Let it go.* Let it go. Gehazi learned his lesson the hard way. Harboring resentment sets us on a path of destruction.

Life Lesson #3: God sees everything. So you can't hide your sin from Him. Gehazi had witnessed Elisha performing miracle after miracle, including raising a young boy from the dead. Yet somehow he thought that Elisha would never find out that he had lied and cheated Naaman out of some clothes and silver. That wasn't very bright of Gehazi, was it? And it's even less bright for you and me to think that we can somehow hide our sin from God. To say it simply: We can't. The LORD sees everything. He sees everything that you *do*. He hears every word that you *speak*, even when you are mumbling under your breath. He even knows every *thought* in your head and every *lust* in your heart. God sees *everything*. So don't make the same mistake that Gehazi made. Don't think: "No one will ever know." God knows, and you can be sure that He will hold you accountable for your sin.

Life Lesson #4: The pleasures of sin are temporary. But God's judgment and God's rewards are eternal. I would love to ask Gehazi the same question I asked the flat-headed little mouse in my mouse trap: Was it worth it? The Bible offers us plenty of examples of individuals who exchanged the eternal blessings of God for a few moments of pleasure. Adam and Eve sacrificed Paradise for a few bites of fruit. Esau sold his birthright for a bowl of porridge. David sacrificed his integrity and favor with God for a one-night stand. And here in 2 Kings 5, Gehazi sacrificed his privileged position as Elisha's servant *and* his own health for two new sets of clothes and some silver coins. There's only one word to describe it: *foolish*.

> Sure, the sin you're considering will bring you a moment's pleasure, but is it worth the cost? Is it really worth it?

Jesus asks his followers a very important question in Matthew 16:26:

> "What good will it be for a man if he gains the whole world, yet forfeits his soul?"
>
> Matthew 16:26

How would Gehazi answer this question: "Was it worth it?" There's no doubt in my mind that he would answer, "Not at all. Not at all."

Friends, as followers of Christ, every one of us needs to think long and hard about the consequences of our sin. We sin because in the moment, sin is fun. But the fun is always short-lived—

temporary. The consequences, however, are eternal. So when a particulary tantalizing temptation lies before you, it would be wise to ask yourself this Gehazi-inspired question, "Is it really worth it?" Sure, the sin you're considering will bring you a moment's pleasure, but is it worth the cost? Is it really worth it? Fievel didn't think so. Gehazi didn't either. And neither will you.

CHAPTER 9

Uzziah, Jotham & Ahaz

A Tale of Three Dads

Some people consider me to be an experienced dad, and for good reason. As the father of four daughters, I've given over ten thousand good night kisses, changed thousands of diapers, prepared hundreds of baby bottles, given a few hundred baths, doled out around one hundred timeouts, and sent three daughters off to kindergarten. If repetition of a task is the best way to master it, then I've mastered a lot of *basic* parenting tasks. So I suppose I can be justifiably labeled "experienced."

But some parents would disagree, saying, "Dane, no dad is truly experienced until he has survived the teenage years. Your job up to this point has been child's play compared to what's up ahead." It seems there's always a joker around who reminds me that because my first three daughters were born within a five-year time span, the time is soon coming when I will have three teenage girls in the house AT THE SAME TIME. Oh no! "Don't remind me," I say. "I'm thinking of buying stock in Midol."

It's true: I have not yet raised a teenager. I've never had a goofy-looking boy show up at my front door holding a corsage on prom night. I've never seen any of my daughters in a cap and gown or walked them down the aisle on their wedding days. And

I am years away from ever hearing a sweet little child look me in the eye and call me "Grandpa."

So there's still so much for me to experience as a dad—so many obstacles to overcome, so many mistakes to make and so many small victories to enjoy. But I know that what will matter most in the years to come is not whether or not I am *experienced*, but instead, whether or not I am *faithful* to the LORD in my role as a dad.

You see, one day after my life here on earth comes to an end, I will have to stand before my LORD and Savior Jesus Christ and give an account of my life. I will have to account for the job I did as a *pastor*. (This weighs heavily on my mind, especially considering the fact that James 3:1 reminds us that "those who teach will be judged more strictly.") I will have to give an account of the job I did as a *husband*. Did I love my wife as Christ loves the church? Did I lead my wife closer to Christ, or did I draw her further from Him?

And certainly, I will be held accountable for the job I did as a *father*. Did I provide for my children? Did I love and nurture them? Did I set a solid, godly example for them? And most importantly, did I lead my kids into a vibrant, enduring relationship with Jesus Christ?

> If a father fails to lead his kids into an abiding relationship with the Savior, he has neglected his most important and most rewarding duty.

As sobering as it may sound, a dad's success or failure is determined more by our answer to this question than any other. A man can be a hard worker, wonderful provider and a loving husband and father. But if he fails to lead his kids into an abiding relationship with the Savior, he has neglected his most important and most rewarding duty.

So dads, we've got our work cut out for us. Whether your kids are five or fifty-five, God has given you a challenging task: Lead your kids to Him. Within the next few pages, we'll observe the examples of three generations of dads: Great Granddad Uzziah, Granddad Jotham and Daddy Ahaz. Each of these men was a king of Judah, which was clearly a very important and influential role in the kingdom. But the Bible allows us to observe these three men in their more *influential* roles—their roles as dads. As we observe their victories and failures, we'll learn some valuable life lessons along the way.

Great Granddaddy Uzziah
(2 Chronicles 26:1-8 & 14-21)

Uzziah (pronounced, "**uh-ZYE-uh**") became king of Judah about one hundred sixty-five years after Israel split into two kingdoms: Israel in the North and Judah in the South. Each of the kings of Judah was a descendant of King David. The LORD had promised David that his descendants would remain on the throne of Israel. And unlike most of the kings in the North, most of Judah's kings did what was right in God's eyes. Uzziah was no exception.

> Then all the people of Judah took Uzziah, who was sixteen years old, and made him king in place of his father Amaziah. He was the one who rebuilt Elath and restored it to Judah after Amaziah rested with his fathers. Uzziah was sixteen years old when he became king, and he reigned in Jerusalem fifty-two years. His mother's name was Jecoliah; she was from Jerusalem. He did what was right in the eyes of the LORD, just as his father Amaziah had done. He sought God during the days of Zechariah, who instructed him in the fear of God. As long as he sought the LORD, God gave him success.
>
> 2 Chronicles 26:1-5

With each of the kings of Judah, the writer of 2 Chronicles sums up his reign by either saying, "He did what was right in the eyes of the LORD" or "He did *not* do what was right in the eyes of the LORD." So we need to ask the question: "What does it mean for one of Judah's kings to have done right in the eyes of the LORD?"

For starters, it means he obeyed God's commands and led others to do the same. Possibly the prophet Micah best summarizes what it means to do what is right in God's eyes.

> He has showed you, O man, what is good. And what does
> the LORD require of you? To act justly and to love mercy
> and to walk humbly with your God.
>
> Micah 6:8

When a man was blessed with the privilege of being king of Judah or Israel, God held that man to a very high standard. The LORD would certainly agree with the wise words of Peter Parker's uncle as Peter was just beginning his transformation into the superhero Spiderman: "With great power comes great responsibility." This statement is especially true when it comes to God's chosen leaders.

The LORD expected Judah's kings to lead with *justice*. He expected His leaders to *extend mercy* to those who were poor, diseased or abused. (God has always had a soft spot in His heart for orphans and widows. This being the case, He has always expected His leaders to treat them with kindness and compassion.) Finally, God expected His appointed kings to walk in humble obedience to His commands. God has no use for big heads or large egos among His leaders.

According to verse 1, Uzziah was placed on the throne at the age of sixteen. Can you imagine if the President of the United States was only sixteen years old? The responsibility of leading a country is too great for a teenager—or so we would think. But Uzziah went on to reign for fifty-two years.

2 Chronicles 26:4 reveals that Uzziah "did what was right in the eyes of the LORD." And the seven words that follow this statement are powerful: "just as his father Amaziah had done." Uzziah followed God and ruled His kingdom with *justice* and *mercy* and *humble obedience*, and this was no accident. He didn't become a godly king by accident. He didn't become

> There are six words that every Christian wants God to say to him/her on Judgment Day: "Well done, good and faithful servant."

a godly king by osmosis. He became a godly king (at least in part) because he had a godly father who set a good example for him.

There are six words that every Christian wants God to say to him/her on Judgment Day: "Well done, good and faithful servant." (See Matthew 25:21.) And for those of us who are parents, our greatest desire should be to have God say the *same* six words to each and every one of our kids on Judgment Day. I can't tell you how *thrilled* I will be if each of my daughters comes through the gates of Heaven, runs up to me and says, "Daddy, Daddy! Guess what Jesus said to me? He looked me in the eye and said, 'Well done, good and faithful servant.'"

There is no doubt that Uzziah's father was a strong, positive influence on his life, but verse 5 reveals a second godly man who influenced him in a profound way, a man named Zechariah. "He sought God during the days of Zechariah, who instructed him in the fear of God. As long as he sought the LORD, God gave him success."

The author of 2 Chronicles clues us in to something very significant here. It wasn't *just* Uzziah's father who kept him following and serving God. Uzziah had a mentor, a man named Zechariah (probably a priest or prophet) who taught him to fear God. In other words, Zechariah taught him to *respect* God, *honor* God and *obey* God. Uzziah obeyed and served the LORD faithfully in large part because he was blessed to have a godly mentor. And I can say with certainty that the LORD has called you to be a similar blessing to younger family members and friends.

Whether or not you are or ever will be a dad, God has called you to be a Zechariah for the next generation of leaders. Christians, do not underestimate God's ability to work through you to be a powerful, godly influence in the lives of the kids, teens and young adults around you. Some of the young people you know have great fathers; others have not-so-great fathers, while still others have no father at all. But you can be a Zechariah in their lives, instructing them in the fear of God.

Well, as Uzziah followed God faithfully during the early years of his reign, God blessed his socks off.

> The Ammonites brought tribute to Uzziah, and his fame spread as far as the border of Egypt, because he had become very powerful. Uzziah built towers in Jerusalem at the Corner Gate, at the Valley Gate and at the angle of the wall, and he fortified them. He also built towers in the desert and dug many cisterns, because he had much livestock in the foothills and in the plain. He had people working his fields and vineyards in the hills and in the fertile lands, for he loved the soil.
>
> 2 Chronicles 26:8-10

Unfortunately, later in his reign, Uzziah's ego grew bigger, and as it did, he started to turn his back on God.

> But after Uzziah became powerful, his pride led to his downfall. He was unfaithful to the LORD his God, and entered the temple of the LORD to burn incense on the altar of incense.
>
> 2 Chronicles 26:16

God had made it very clear to the Jewish people that only *priests* were permitted to burn incense in the temple. But in his pride, Uzziah thought that he was above the law, and the rules didn't apply to him. He was wrong. The LORD punished Uzziah swiftly. He struck him with a skin disease (some variation of leprosy) that demanded quarantine. He had to live in seclusion in a separate house for the rest of his life, which precluded him from leading effectively. As a result, he had to hand over his kingdom to his son Jotham.

Granddaddy Jotham
(2 Chronicles 27:1-9)

The second dad we're going to observe is Uzziah's son: Granddaddy Jotham (pronounced, "**JOH-thuhm**").

> Jotham was twenty-five years old when he became king, and he reigned in Jerusalem sixteen years. His mother's name was Jerusha daughter of Zadok. He did what was right in the eyes of the LORD, just as his father Uzziah had done, but unlike him he did not enter the temple of the LORD. The people, however, continued their corrupt practices....Jotham grew powerful because he walked steadfastly before the LORD his God.
>
> 2 Chronicles 27:1-2, 6

In verse 2 we once again read these encouraging words: "He did what was right in the eyes of the LORD just as his father Uzziah had done." But then comes another point in Jotham's favor: "but unlike him he did not enter the temple of the LORD." There are few joys in this life greater than the joy of a father witnessing his kids following in his footsteps…the *good* footsteps. We want our kids to follow our good example without repeating our dumb mistakes.

As we look back over our lives, there are many pitfalls of sin that we fell into that we want our kids to avoid. We don't want our kids to fall headlong into an addiction to drugs or alcohol. We don't want our kids to get entangled in pornography or sexual perversion. We don't want our kids to get caught up in the pitfalls of credit cards, get-rich-quick schemes and materialism that lead to financial ruin. And we certainly don't want our kids to stray from God as many of us did.

> We want our kids to follow our good example without repeating our dumb mistakes.

Don't we want our kids to *learn from* our mistakes and not to *repeat* them? And here in 2 Chronicles 27, we see the pattern that we hope and pray our kids will follow. Jotham followed in his dad's *godly* footsteps, but he avoided Uzziah's footsteps that were outside God's will. As a result, "Jotham grew powerful because he walked steadfastly before the LORD his God."

There is only one fault that we can find with Jotham here in chapter 27. According to verse 2: "The people, however, continued their corrupt practices." Jotham is a great example of a leader who led *himself* toward godliness but didn't take his followers with him. One of the simplest definitions of leadership is: *influence.* God had given Jotham the most powerful position of influence in the nation of Judah, but Jotham missed the opportunity to lead his people to do what was right in the eyes of the LORD.

He made a grave mistake that we dare not make ourselves. You see, whether or not you realize it, you *are* a person of influence.

At work: Whether you are a top level executive or the lowest level employee, your presence at work influences others. So you need to ask yourself: "What kind of influence am I having on my employees/coworkers?"

At church: Whether you are a pastor, a volunteer or just a casual attender, your presence at church influences others. Ask yourself, "What kind of influence am I having on others at church?"

Among your friends: Whether you're an introvert or extrovert, a party animal or a wallflower, a born leader or a content follower, your influence on your friends is greater than you realize. So ask yourself, "What kind of influence am I having on my friends?"

Well, Jotham missed a golden opportunity to lead his people to do what was right in God's eyes. Worse still, we learn in the following chapter (2 Chronicles 28) that Jotham's own son, Ahaz (pronounced, "**AY-haz**"), grew up to be a wicked man. Jotham clearly did *not* lead his own son to do what was right in the eyes of the LORD.

Daddy Ahaz
(2 Chronicles 28:1-5 & 22-27)

It's apparent from 2 Chronicles 28:1-4 that Ahaz was an evil king, even stooping so low as to throw his own sons into sacrificial fires to false gods:

> Ahaz was twenty years old when he became king, and he reigned in Jerusalem sixteen years. Unlike David his father, he did not do what was right in the eyes of the LORD. He walked in the ways of the kings of Israel and also made cast idols for worshiping the Baals. He burned sacrifices in the Valley of Ben Hinnom and sacrificed his sons in the fire, following the detestable ways of the nations the LORD had driven out before the Israelites. He offered sacrifices and burned incense at the high places, on the hilltops and under every spreading tree.
>
> 2 Chronicles 28:1-4

The wording is very interesting in verse 1. Ahaz was thirteen generations removed from King David. King David was his great, great, great, great, great, great, great, great, great, great, great grandfather. Yet David, not Jotham, was held up in Israel as the model of a godly king.

I don't know about you, but that kind of multi-generational influence inspires me. How about this for a challenge: Live such a godly life that it inspires the next thirteen generations of your grandchildren? (Personally, I think Jesus will return sooner than that. But if He doesn't, it would be inspiring to know that my example is rippling through the ages of time from generation to generation.) Our names will likely be forgotten after we die, but hopefully our examples will impact many generations to come.

> **How about this for a challenge: Live such a godly life that it inspires the next thirteen generations of your grandchildren?**

Unfortunately, Jotham didn't pass on his godly example to his son Ahaz, and as a result, Ahaz became one of the most wicked kings in Judah's history. He turned his back on the LORD and began to serve idols instead. As verse 23 makes clear, the result of his idol worship was disastrous for both Ahaz and his nation.

> He offered sacrifices to the gods of Damascus, who had defeated him; for he thought, "Since the gods of the kings of Aram have helped them, I will sacrifice to them so they will help me." But they were his downfall and the downfall of all Israel.
>
> 2 Chronicles 28:23

When all was said and done, the blame for Ahaz's heinous, immoral behavior rested squarely on his own shoulders. The Bible is quite clear that each of us is personally responsible for our own sin. On Judgment Day when we stand before the LORD and give an account of our lives, we won't have the luxury of passing on the blame. We won't be able to say, "My sin was my parents' fault!" or "My ex-wife drove me to my breaking point!" We won't even be able to get away with saying, "The devil made me do it!" The LORD is a strong believer in personal responsibility.

However, at the same time God emphasizes in His word the powerful role that parents occupy—a role of starting their kids on the path of making wise and godly choices. Deuteronomy 6 contains one of the central teachings of the Old Testament. Jewish rabbis refer to the passage beginning in verse 4 as the "shema," the core of the Mosaic Law:

> On Judgment Day when we stand before the LORD and give an account of our lives, we won't have the luxury of passing on the blame.

Hear, O Israel: The LORD our God, the LORD is one. Love the LORD your God with all your heart and with all your soul and with all your strength. These commandments that I give you today are to be upon your hearts. Impress them on your children. Talk about them when you sit at home and when you walk along the road, when you lie down and when you get up. Tie them as symbols on your hands and bind them on your foreheads. Write them on the doorframes of your houses and on your gates.

Deuteronomy 6:4-9

There is no possibility of overstating the great influence that parents have on their children. Ultimately, God held Ahaz responsible for his *own* sin. But we can be certain that God also held Jotham accountable for failing to impress God's love and laws upon his son's heart.

Now, since Ahaz was a wicked man who set a wicked example, we would expect him to have a wicked son. Right? But we read something surprising about Ahaz's son Hezekiah in 2 Chronicles 29:2. Hezekiah actually "did what was right in the eyes of the LORD, just as his father David had done." It turns out that Hezekiah was one of the best kings that Israel ever had. Hezekiah was zealous for the LORD and for His laws. Does that mean that Ahaz was a *good* dad who set him a *good* example? Not at all! This was a case where a son became a godly man *in spite of* his dad's crummy example.

3 Life Lessons

Life Lesson #1: A Lesson from Great Granddaddy Uzziah: Aim to be a consistent, godly influence in your home. Don't allow your selfish pride to lead to your downfall. One of the axioms I try to live by is this one: *End well.* So often in life we encounter a man or woman who serves the LORD faithfully for an extended period of time but then loses his/her drive and backs away from ministry.

Now, there are plenty of times when Christians of great impact have to step away from ministry because of health or family issues. These are not the Christians I have in mind. I'm concerned about those who *have served* the LORD faithfully in the past and have the potential to serve Him faithfully today but for whatever reason, choose not to do so. Friend, if you have served the LORD faithfully in the past, way to go! Don't quit! Don't let up! Like Paul, keep pressing on toward the spiritual finish line. Run life's race as if the gold medal awaits you (see Philippians 3:14). Keep serving the LORD faithfully until your dying day. End well!

Life Lesson #2: A Lesson from Granddaddy Jotham: Walk in your dad's *good* footsteps. Avoid his *bad* footsteps, but don't forget to lead your own children to choose the right path. Over the past few years, I have noticed a disturbing trend among the most godly men in the Bible: Quite often, they are lousy dads. Isn't that sad? Godly men like Jacob, Eli, Samuel, David, Hezekiah and Josiah had wicked sons.

Certainly there are times when a godly father fulfills his God-given duty to teach the love and laws of the LORD to his children and they rebel, choosing the path of wickedness anyway. Unfortunately, this was not the case with the aforementioned fathers. Each of them dropped the ball. They poured their time and effort into many admirable duties, but they neglected the greatest of duties: to lead their children to the LORD. For example, Eli served as Israel's high priest, but he refused to discipline his two rebellious sons, Hophni and Phineas (1 Samuel 2:12-36). David was "a man after God's own heart," but he didn't even talk with his treacherous son Absalom for five years (2 Samuel 13:38; 2 Samuel 14:28). How could he teach Absalom to follow God when he wasn't even talking to him? And Josiah, although he was one of the most godly kings in Judah's history, had not one but *two* sons who became king after his death, and both were rebellious and wicked.

As a *son*, Jotham was a great role model. He followed his dad's godly example while sidestepping his dad's failures. But as a *father*, Jotham was a poor role model. He failed to pass on his faith to his son, and as a result, both Jotham and his kingdom suffered a disastrous outcome. Therefore, every Christian man should aim to be a two-fold role model: a godly son *and* a godly father.

Life Lesson #3: A Lesson from Daddy Ahaz: Don't cross your fingers and hope that your children won't follow your bad example. If your kids follow God as adults, it should be *because* of you not *in spite* of you. Being a father is a 24/7 job. And as every parent knows, our kids tend to mimic our bad behaviors more quickly than they mimic our good behaviors. A few years ago, a friend of mine lamented that his four-year-old daughter had blurted out a four-letter word one day, a word that she had learned from *him*. The word had slipped out innocently enough. He had to slam on his brakes at an intersection to avoid a reckless driver, and out came the "sh-bomb." All it took was one time, and his daughter's little mental sponge soaked it up.

I have prayed many times that my daughters will grow to have twice the faith in Christ and twice the influence in this world that I have. Once again, my greatest responsibility as a Christian dad is to ensure that I am leading each of my daughters into a vibrant relationship with Jesus Christ. Parents, you've chosen to follow Christ. Fantastic! Now lead your kids to do the same. At times you may have dropped the ball as your family's spiritual leader, but with the time you have left...*end well.*

> I have prayed many times that my daughters will grow to have twice the faith in Christ and twice the influence in this world that I have.

As your kids come to maturity, they will make their own decisions about whether or not to follow Christ, but it is *your* duty and privilege to do everything within your power to pave the way for them to make the *right* decision, the decision for which they will be eternally grateful. I hope and pray that each of your children will make the decision to follow Christ—not *in spite* of you but *because* of you. So leave a legacy for your children and grandchildren: a legacy of following Christ well.

CHAPTER 10

Hilkiah, Shaphan & Huldah

They Paved the Way for Revival

When my wife, Christine, and I discovered in the spring of 2001 that she was expecting, we were ecstatic. My wife broke the news to me by giving me a gift bag that contained two cute baby outfits: one blue and one pink. From the very first day the question was raised: "Do you think we'll have a boy or a girl?" Our minds began to play out the two possible scenarios.

Like most couples, as the first trimester came and went we discussed whether or not we should find out the baby's gender ahead of time. For us the decision was easy. Christine was anxious to shop for baby clothes, and we were more than a little bit impatient. So we opted for the sneak preview. As the day of Christine's second trimester ultrasound appointment approached, we continued to play the guessing game.

As we drove together to the obstetrician's office on that warm fall day, I had a hunch that my wife was having a boy. To be honest with you, my hunch was less of a premonition than it was a preference. Deep down I wanted a boy because I was *scared* to have a girl. As the youngest child in my family, I had never had the experience of preparing a bottle, giving a bath or even changing a diaper. But at least as a man I felt that I knew a thing or two about being *male*. But raising a girl—I felt completely unprepared for a task like that. And there were certain things about raising a daughter that scared me to death: namely, teenage boys.

But as we left the doctor's office that day after having heard the news, "It's a girl," I had just a few short months to come to grips with the reality of being a little girl's daddy. Even though I felt completely ill-equipped and unprepared, I realized that God knew what He was doing. He was a better family planner than me, so I would trust Him and try my best to be the best "girl daddy" I could possibly be.

Over the next eight years I had three more chances to predict the gender of our babies. Just as I had with my wife's first pregnancy, I had a hunch. Each time my hunch was that we were having a boy. And wouldn't you know it? Every single time I was wrong. Not in a million years would I have imagined having four daughters. I had doubts about raising *one* daughter, but the LORD gave me four! Still today I marvel at the thought: I have four girls. What a blessing! What a responsibility!

Because I believe that my greatest duty as a father is to lead my girls into a vibrant relationship with Jesus Christ, I need all the help I can get. Without a doubt, I need *God's* help. I also need the help of my wife. (My girls need the steady example of a godly mother.) And as I teach them God's word, I'm so grateful for the shining examples of godly women like Esther, Ruth, Mary and Huldah (pronounced, "**HOOL-duh**").

Huldah is one of my all-time favorite unknown characters in the Old Testament. In fact, I like Huldah so much that for the last few years I've been trying to convince mothers-to-be to name their baby girls "Huldah." My argument usually goes something like this:

"Think about it: The name Huldah sounds like a Viking warrior princess or a Swedish bouncer. I bet you've never heard of anyone mugging a girl named Huldah. Right? When I think about the name Huldah, I picture a woman who can pick up a man with her bare hands and toss him through a window. She'd be a great lady to have around. The ADT salesman knocks on your door: 'Hey, can I interest you in a security system for your home?' 'Nope! Don't need one,' you respond. 'I've got Huldah!'"

I think that my sales pitch has been top notch. But so far, I haven't had any takers. Maybe *you* can be the first.

Over the next few pages we'll turn to 2 Chronicles 34 to take a closer look at Huldah, along with two other little-known fellows whose stories are woven into her story: Hilkiah (pronounced, **"hil-KIE-uh"**) and Shaphan (pronounced, **"SHAY-fuhn"**). During a period of moral decline, these two men and one woman were used by God to help usher in a great spiritual revival in Judah—a revival that positively and powerfully impacted tens of thousands of lives.

Good King Josiah

In 2 Chronicles 34:1, we read that Josiah became king of Judah at the tender age of eight. Even though Josiah's dad and granddad were both wicked men, Josiah became a very good and godly king who led his country back to the LORD. In 2 Chronicles 34:2 we read the oft-repeated words that are music to our ears when reading a description of an Israelite king:

> He did what was right in the eyes of the LORD and walked in the ways of his father David, not turning to the right or to the left.
>
> 2 Chronicles 34:2

As we continue reading, we quickly discover that this very young king had a very big heart for God.

> In the eighth year of his reign, while he was still young, he began to seek the God of his father David.

2 Chronicles 34:3a

If you do some quick math, you discover that Josiah was just fifteen or sixteen years old. As a young teenager, Josiah began seeking the LORD. To me, this is so inspiring. Who says that a teenager is too young to seek after God? Josiah did it, and the teenagers we know can do it as well. Isn't it a blessing to know that God's word spotlights several teen heroes, like Josiah, that the young people in our lives can look up to and emulate?

By the age of sixteen, Josiah was seeking after God, but his teenage exploits for the LORD had only just begun.

| This very young king had a very big heart for God.

In his twelfth year [as king] he began to purge Judah and Jerusalem of high places, Asherah poles, carved idols and cast images.

2 Chronicles 34:3b

So how old was Josiah at this point? He was nineteen or twenty! Who says that a college student can't be used of God to transform culture? In verses 4-7 we're given a detailed description of how thorough Josiah's housecleaning was.

Under his direction the altars of the Baals were torn down; he cut to pieces the incense altars that were above them, and smashed the Asherah poles, the idols and the images. These he broke to pieces and scattered over the graves of those who had sacrificed to them. He burned the bones of the priests on their altars, and so he purged Judah and Jerusalem. In the towns of Manasseh, Ephraim and Simeon, as far as Naphtali, and in the ruins around them, he tore down the altars and the Asherah poles and crushed the idols to powder and cut to pieces all the incense altars throughout Israel. Then he went back to Jerusalem.

2 Chronicles 34:4-7

Josiah's task was no small feat, because people tend to be very attached to their prized possessions. Imagine someone taking a sledgehammer to your car or a baseball bat to your flat screen television. Would you feel like blowing your top? Many in Judah must have felt the same way, kicking and screaming as Josiah's men tore down objects of worship all around the country. But Josiah was not swayed. Regardless of the backlash, Josiah tore down the idols anyway.

By the age of nineteen, King Josiah had already made some remarkable changes in Judah, but true revival had not yet

> When the temple was in physical shambles, inevitably, the nation of Israel was in spiritual shambles.

come. In verse 8 we read that in the eighteenth year of Josiah's reign, at the age of twenty-five, he ordered three of his key political leaders to see to it that the temple was completely repaired. And because of their tireless efforts, the temple was purified of all remnants of idolatry and became fully operational for the first time in years.

This was a top priority for King Josiah, because when the temple was in *physical* shambles, inevitably, the nation of Israel was in *spiritual* shambles. When the temple suffered physical neglect, the LORD experienced spiritual neglect. Because King Josiah was a man whose greatest desire was to please God, he was not going to stand for this neglect any longer.

Josiah accomplished quite a bit before the age of twenty-six. Wouldn't you agree? Yet his greatest work for the LORD was still to come. The next section of 2 Chronicles 34 reveals one of the greatest discoveries in the Bible: the Bible itself. It was a discovery that happened on Josiah's watch, and it is here that we are introduced to Hilkiah, Shaphan and Huldah.

A Prelude to Revival

While they were bringing out the money that had been taken into the temple of the LORD, Hilkiah the priest found the Book of the Law of the LORD that had been given through Moses. Hilkiah said to Shaphan the secretary, "I have found the Book of the Law in the temple of the LORD." He gave it to Shaphan. Then Shaphan took the book to the king and reported to him: "Your officials are doing everything that has been committed to them. They have paid out the money that was in the temple of the LORD and have entrusted it to the supervisors and workers." Then Shaphan the secretary informed the king, "Hilkiah the priest has given me a book." And Shaphan read from it in the presence of the king.

2 Chronicles 34:14-18

Imagine the scene. The beautiful gold temple that Solomon had built three hundred years earlier was in a state of disrepair. The glimmer of the gold was gone; the stones were cracked; the wood beams were dried out and splintered; there were cobwebs in the corners of the rooms and dust on the floors. And worst of all, signs of idolatry were everywhere. God's house was in dire need of some spring cleaning and renovations, and Josiah made sure the work got done.

As Hilkiah the high priest was keeping an eye on the work that was being done, he discovered something tucked away in the temple. He found the Book of the Law (most likely the Book of Deuteronomy and possibly Leviticus and Numbers as well). One of the priests had probably hidden these scriptures during the reign of one of the evil kings who hated God's word.

So what did Hilkiah do with this treasure he had just found? According to verse 15, he gave it to the king's secretary, a man named Shaphan. And Shaphan responded by doing something that made a profound impact on both the king and his kingdom: He took the Book of the Law to Josiah and read it to him.

By rabbinic count, there are 613 laws contained in the Books of the Law (Genesis, Exodus, Leviticus, Numbers and Deuteronomy) that the Jewish people were required to obey. If Shaphan read from only a portion of these five books, he probably read through a few hundred of these laws. Josiah's heart sank and his countenance changed as Shaphan read law after law after law. And he was filled with both remorse and fear as Shaphan read passages like this one:

> For you are a people holy to the LORD your God. The LORD your God has chosen you out of all the peoples on the face of the earth to be His people, His treasured possession. The LORD did not set His affection on you and choose you because you were more numerous than other peoples, for you were the fewest of all peoples. But it was because the LORD loved you and kept the oath He swore to your forefathers that He brought you out with a mighty hand and redeemed you from the land of slavery, from the power of Pharoah king of Egypt. Know therefore that the LORD your God is God; He is the faithful God, keeping His covenant of love to a thousand generations of those who love Him and keep His commands. But those who hate Him He will repay to their face by destruction; He will not be slow to repay to their face those who hate Him. Therefore, take care to follow the commands, decrees and laws I give you today.
>
> Deuteronomy 7:6-11

Because Josiah had a soft heart for God, his response was immediate:

> When the king heard the words of the Law, he tore his robes. He gave these orders to Hilkiah, Ahikam son of Shaphan, Abdon son of Micah, Shaphan the secretary and Asaiah the king's attendant: "Go and inquire of the LORD for me and for the remnant in Israel and Judah about what is written in this book that has been found. Great is the LORD's anger that is poured out on us because our fathers have not kept the word of the LORD; they have not acted in accordance with all that is written in this book."
>
> 2 Chronicles 34:19-21

For the first time in his life, Josiah's mind and heart were exposed to the pure, unadulterated truth of God's word. The eyes of his heart were opened to the reality that Israel was set apart as "holy to the LORD." Out of all the nations on earth God had "chosen" Israel to be "His treasured possession," not because Israel was a large or impressive nation, but simply because the LORD "loved" Israel. Josiah's eyes were opened to the depth of God's love, but at the same time he came to understand that sinning against God is *hatred* toward God. And the LORD would respond to His people's hatred with swift destruction.

> For the first time in his life, Josiah's mind and heart were exposed to the pure, unadulterated truth of God's word.

In response to these revelations from God's word, Josiah did something to demonstrate great sorrow and repentance: He tore his robes and ordered five of his top leaders to find out what the LORD wanted him to do in response. And it's at this point that we are introduced to my favorite Swedish bouncer...Huldah.

Hilkiah and those the king had sent with him went to speak to the prophetess Huldah, who was the wife of Shallum son of Tokhath, the son of Hasrah, keeper of the wardrobe. She lived in Jerusalem, in the Second District.

2 Chronicles 34:22

Surprisingly, Huldah is not introduced as a bouncer *or* a warrior princess. She's introduced as something more remarkable: a prophetess. Just when we think we have God all figured out, He throws us a curveball. Although most prophets in the Bible are *male*, we do read of several prophetesses in the Bible, including Moses' sister Miriam in Exodus 15:20 and Deborah in Judges 4:4. So Huldah is in good company.

Once you come to terms with the reality that God set Huldah apart as a prophetess, take a few moments to process this puzzling fact: Huldah was a contemporary of the much-better-known prophets Jeremiah and Zephaniah. Both of these godly men were prophesying in Israel during the reign of Josiah. Jeremiah went on to write two books in the Old Testament (Jeremiah and Lamentations), and Zephaniah wrote the Book of Zephaniah.

So with this in mind, I have an important question: If both Jeremiah and Zephaniah were alive and prophesying in Josiah's day, why on earth did Hilkiah and his buddies go to see Huldah instead? If a master brain surgeon is available to perform a life-saving brain surgery on a family member, we wouldn't opt for a medical intern to operate, would we? And if we have to rely on another driver to get us to our destination, wouldn't we choose a driver with years of driving experience and a spotless driving record over a sixteen-year-old who just got his learner's permit?

I find it curious that the Jewish high priest would seek God's counsel from an otherwise unknown prophetess instead of from these two prophetic power houses. At this point Jeremiah and Zephaniah were in the early years of their prophetic ministries.

Even still, why would they choose Huldah? I've given this question some thought over the past few years, and I'm still a bit stumped. Maybe the two big boys were on vacation at the time. Or perhaps they were on assignment elsewhere. I can only speculate.

All I can say with certainty is this: Hilkiah and his fellow leaders chose Huldah because *God* had chosen Huldah. She was the one whom the LORD had chosen to communicate *His* word to *His* people at *this* time. Regardless of her obscurity, regardless of her gender and regardless of her funny name, God had chosen *her*. Ultimately, that's all that mattered.

A *priest* speaks to God on behalf of the people. A *prophet* speaks to the people on behalf of God. Hilkiah was a very knowledgeable and godly priest, but he was ill-equipped to prophesy. He needed Huldah, and in verses 22-28 she delivered the LORD's message that Josiah desperately needed to hear. It was a message that included both judgment for sin and reward for righteousness.

> A priest speaks to God on behalf of the people. A prophet/prophetess speaks to the people on behalf of God.

She said to them, "This is what the LORD, the God of Israel, says: Tell the man who sent you to me, 'This is what the LORD says: I am going to bring disaster on this place and its people – all the curses written in the book that has been read in the presence of the king of Judah. Because they have forsaken Me and burned incense to other gods and provoked Me to anger by all that their hands have made, My anger will be poured out on this place and will not be quenched.' Tell the king of Judah, who sent you to inquire of the LORD, 'This is what the LORD, the God of Israel, says concerning the words you heard. Because your heart was responsive and you humbled yourself before God when you heard what He spoke against this place and its people, and because you humbled yourself before

Me and tore your robes and wept in My presence, I have heard you, declares the LORD. Now I will gather you to your fathers, and you will be buried in peace. Your eyes will not see all the disaster I am going to bring on this place and on those who live here.'" So they took her answer back to the king.

2 Chronicles 34:23-28

The LORD's message delivered through Huldah contained both bad news and good news. The *bad* news was that God was determined to bring "disaster" on the people of Judah. He would pour out on Judah all the curses promised to disobedient sinners in the Book of the Law. The LORD's anger would *not* be quenched.

However, the *good* news was that God was going to spare Josiah the misery of witnessing this judgment during his lifetime. Because Josiah had responded to God's laws with a soft, humble heart and had torn his robes and wept in His presence, the LORD was going to bless Josiah for his righteousness. God would allow him to live out the remainder of his days in peace. The LORD's judgment upon Judah would surely come, but not until after Josiah's death.

In verse 28 Hilkiah and company relayed the LORD's message to King Josiah, and he once again responded with humility. He summoned all of Judah's elders, went to the temple and read God's word to the people of Jerusalem who had gathered. And after he finished reading God's laws, he led his people in a fresh pledge to God. The people renewed their covenant with God, promising to follow Him with all their hearts and souls and obey His commands written in the Book of the Law.

In the final verse of the chapter (verse 33), we discover that Josiah purged Israel of all the idols that had been set up by prior kings. And "He had all who were present in Israel serve the LORD their God. As long as he lived they did not fail to follow the LORD, the God of their fathers." Way to go, Josiah! He followed the LORD faithfully throughout his lifetime, and he led his people to do the same. Revival had come to Judah.

4 Life Lessons

Life Lesson #1: A Lesson from Hilkiah and Shaphan: The greatest buried treasure you'll ever find is God's word, and it's a treasure that must be read and shared. What a tragedy it would have been if Hilkiah had never discovered the Book of the Law. For years God's word had sat hidden and neglected underneath a pile of clutter in the temple. And sadly, the same could be said about the Bible in many of our homes and churches today.

Two of my favorite verses about the importance of the Bible are 2 Timothy 3:16-17 and Hebrews 4:12.

> All Scripture is God-breathed and is useful for teaching, rebuking, correcting and training in righteousness, so that the man of God may be thoroughly equipped for every good work.
>
> 2 Timothy 3:16-17

Isn't that remarkable? The Bible is "God-breathed." The Bible is useful for teaching, useful for rebuking and correcting, and useful for training and equipping us for "every good work." The Bible is in a class by itself—the only book on the planet that can rightly claim to be "God-breathed." The writer of Hebrews even describes the Bible as being alive:

> For the word of God is living and active. Sharper than any double-edged sword, it penetrates even to dividing soul and spirit, joints and marrow; it judges the thoughts and attitudes of the heart.
>
> Hebrews 4:12

Taken together, these verses in 2 Timothy and Hebrews describe the Bible more as a *living being* than as a document. The Bible is both God-breathed and alive.

So let me ask you: Would you ever place your dog or cat on a bookshelf and let it gather dust? Of course not! "Sit, Fido, sit! I'll pull you off the shelf and dust you off when I get around to it… maybe on Christmas or Easter." And you would never neglect your own children (or someone else's, for that matter) in the corner of a room for a few months or years, would you? "I saw some kids at the store today, and seeing them reminded me that I have two kids of my own. I forgot I left them in their bedroom a few months ago."

> Today is the day to restore God's word to its proper place in your life and household.

Of course these examples are ridiculous, but I'm sure you understand where I'm going with this. If you wouldn't let your dog, cat or children gather dust underneath a pile of clutter, why would you allow the living, breathing word of God to do so? Thank God for Hilkiah and Shaphan, who wisely dusted off the Book of the Law, read it and shared it with the king. We would do well to follow in their footsteps. If your Bible has been gathering dust in recent months, today is the day to pick it up, dust it off, read it and share it with others. Today is the day to restore God's word to its proper place in your life and household.

Life Lesson #2: A Lesson from Josiah: When confronted by the truth of God's word, your *heart* must be responsive, your *spirit* must be humble, and your *actions* should demonstrate repentance. Most kings wouldn't have done what Josiah did. Several years later when Jehoiakim was king of Judah, the prophet Jeremiah delivered some written prophesies that declared God's word to him. King Jehoiakim didn't like what the LORD had to say, so he cut the biblical scroll into pieces and threw them into a fire (Jeremiah 36:23). Although most people these days would not go so far as to *burn* God's word, many are just as quick as Jehoiakim to harden their hearts and reject it.

But we must follow in Josiah's footsteps. We must be ready and willing to *receive* God's correction and rebuke. In fact, like King David, we should *invite* it.

> Search me, O God, and know my heart; test me and know my anxious thoughts. See if there is any offensive way in me, and lead me in the way everlasting.
>
> Psalm 139:23-24

If we are not humble, we are of very little use to God. And if we are unwilling to repent, then we can *not* experience the LORD's mercy and grace. Josiah shines as a powerful example of a man whose humility allowed God to

> If we are not humble, we are of very little use to God.

transform a nation through him, and his repentance paved the way for a revival in Judah. So be humble and penitent before God. He always makes it worth your while.

Life Lesson #3: A Lesson from Huldah: Regardless of your gender, your age or how strange your name may sound, people will seek your counsel if they know you'll speak God's truth. When I became a full-time pastor, I was only twenty-five years old. Several months into my ministry, the question came to mind: What was I thinking when I took this job? It wasn't that I didn't enjoy being a pastor or was being treated poorly. I just felt inadequate for the task. After all, in a church with quite a few seniors, I was preaching each Sunday to men and women who had been Christians twice as long as I'd been alive. What could I possibly teach them?

But the LORD quickly revealed to me that regardless of my age or lack of life experience, I had much to teach the people in the congregation as long as I taught them God's word. His word was older than the oldest member of our church, and its wisdom was wiser than the wisest person in the church. As long as I consistently taught His word accurately, my teaching would be authoritative and filled with spiritual wisdom.

In ancient Jewish culture, most females did not enjoy the liberties and privileges that men did. But that didn't stop the high priest and the king's associates from seeking Huldah's counsel. When it came down to it, Huldah's gender, physical characteristics, IQ and socio-economic status were secondary issues. Of primary concern was her ability to consistently and accurately speak God's word. The same is true for you and me today. If you, like Huldah, become known as one who faithfully speaks God's word, those with soft and humble hearts *will* listen.

Life Lesson #4: A Lesson from Judah: Even after a great revival, God's judgment may still fall upon a nation. Sadly, within twenty years of the discovery of the Book of the Law and the revival that followed it, God's promised judgment began to fall upon Judah. During the reign of Josiah's son Jehoiakim, the mighty army of Babylon swept into Jerusalem and captured the city. It was the first of three Babylonian invasions that would strike Judah over a twenty-year period.

The fact is, prior to Josiah's ascension to the throne, Judah had already crossed a spiritual line in the sand that had sealed her fate. The people's sin had mushroomed to such an extent that God's judgment *must* fall upon the nation. Even the godly Josiah could not alter this divine imperative.

With this in mind, I've wondered in recent years if the United States of America has crossed a similar line in the sand. I am convinced that a major spiritual revival is on the horizon, a revival that will sweep through churches like wildfire, setting the faith of

Christians ablaze and resulting in the salvation of millions of unbelievers across the country. I have been praying for revival for over thirteen years, and I am convinced it's coming in the near future. Yet I wonder…even if such a revival turns our nation back to God, will it be too late? Have we, like Judah, already crossed a spiritual threshold? Will God's judgment fall upon our country anyway?

If we have not yet passed the point of no return, it's clear that we are quickly moving in that direction. Therefore, I hold out hope that there are enough Christians in this country who will cry out to God for a revival that will turn the tide. I hold out hope that there are enough of us who are serious about rediscovering God's word like Hilkiah, humbly repenting of our sins like Josiah and boldly speaking God's true word like Huldah. If there are, there is great hope for our nation, and there is great hope for our world. Won't you be one of many who joins the ranks of Hilkiah, Shaphan and Huldah, paving the way for revival?

> I hold out hope that there are enough Christians in this country who will cry out to God for a revival that will turn the tide.

AFTERWARD

Seventeen obscure heroes and villains, thirty-five life lessons, and fourteen hundred years of biblical history—I'd say we've covered a good bit of ground together. We've gotten better acquainted with the Old Testament. We've met plenty of little-known characters most people overlook or ignore. And we've discovered some wonderful, unusual names that deserve to be added to our book of baby names. Shiphrah, Puah, Peninnah, Gehazi, Shimei and Huldah—you have to admit that these are some great-sounding names. We've had a lot of fun on this journey together, haven't we?

But this journey was never intended to be for entertainment purposes only. This journey was intended to be life-changing. I believe the LORD wanted you to meet these obscure men and women and be changed by them. So I encourage you to go to God in prayer and ask Him, *Father, how do you want me to respond to what I've read? Reveal to me where my life is lacking and which life lessons I need to start living out today.*

I believe He will answer your heartfelt prayer as you flip back through the pages and review the life lessons in each chapter. Some of these lessons probably didn't convict you when you first read them, and they won't convict you when you read them again. But you will discover that as you review them with a spirit of humble teachability, certain lessons will hit you square between the eyes. Rest assured, my friend, you are not alone. Many of these life lessons I've shared *are* hard-hitting. If some of them slap you upside the head, they quite likely have slapped many others (including me) upside the head as well.

The LORD has convicted me with many of these lessons in the past, and He will continue to convict me with them and others in years to come. For example, I'm convicted by the reality that if push came to shove, I'm not certain that I would stand up to intimidation and threats as well as Shiphrah, Puah or Micaiah. And I can't guarantee that I will successfully sidestep all of the parenting pitfalls into which Uzziah, Jotham and Ahaz fell.

Like you, I am imperfect. I fail. I don't live up to God's perfect standards, and I let people down. Like you, I am a work in progress. And as such, God has used each of the aforementioned "nobodies" to help make sure my progress continues. He has used these men and women to help conform me to the image of his Son: Jesus Christ. Certainly this is God's desire for you as well.

The LORD has made it clear in His word that before the beginning of time, He determined for you to be conformed to the image of Jesus so that you could lead many others to Him (Romans 8:29). This being the case, over the course of your life, the LORD has used thousands of people, situations, victories, failures, friends, enemies, sermons and books to patiently and methodically conform you to the image of Christ.

And it is my hope and prayer that this book is one of the tools in His hand to continue the process in you. So I encourage you to let Him work. If Jesus Christ is your Lord, let Him use this book in your life every bit as much as He wants to. If He leads you back to a certain chapter, follow His lead and let Him do His work of rebuking, correcting and training you. If He leads you to point a family member or friend to a certain chapter, character or life lesson, do it. While the Holy Spirit draws you to certain characters and life lessons, He will likely

> Over the course of your life, the LORD has used thousands of people, situations, victories, failures, friends, enemies, sermons and books to patiently and methodically conform you to the image of Christ.

draw your family members and friends to completely different ones. And at a different season of your life, He will likely point *you* to different characters and lessons. God works in each of us in His *perfect* way at the *perfect* time. God is so good!

1 Final Life Lesson

Now, I've saved the most important life lesson for last, and this lesson is not from an obscure, unknown character in the Old Testament but from the central character in the whole Bible: Jesus Christ.

A Lesson from Jesus Christ: "I am the way and the truth and the life. No one comes to the Father except through me" (John 14:6). If you are reading this book right now, you have, at the very least, a curiosity about spiritual things. But your curiosity won't get you into Heaven when you die. Contrary to popular belief, not even good works, religion or church attendance will get you into Heaven. There is only one way to get there, and Jesus Christ *is* the "one way." In this day and age, this reality seems narrow-minded. Nevertheless, it's true. Like it or not, Jesus *is* the only way. Oftentimes, I say it this way: There is only one way to get to Heaven, and that's to follow Jesus there.

The Bible is very clear that your *good works* won't get you into Heaven, because good works are powerless to erase the sins that separate you from God. In fact, because God is perfectly holy and just, His character demands the spiritual death penalty for your sins. That's what Hell is…the spiritual death penalty. Hell is eternal separation from God, which brings with it eternal darkness, fear, agony and hopelessness. The bad news is…because you have rebelled against your Creator and broken His perfect laws over and over again, you will be separated from God for eternity in Hell—unless someone takes your place.

The good news is...Jesus *is* that someone. Two thousand years ago Jesus took your place. He carried out the death penalty for you. He sat down in the eternal electric chair; He stepped in front of the celestial firing squad; He took the lethal injection of Hell that *you* deserved. And He did it all because God loved you so much (John 3:16; Romans 5:8). Jesus' death on the cross for your sins was God's greatest gift of love from Him to you. By taking the death penalty for you, He has offered you a full and complete acquittal from your sins. He has offered you the opportunity to have your sin-debt paid in full so that you can be set free to live life to the fullest here on Earth and live eternally with God in Heaven. That's a fantastic gift of grace, isn't it?

But God does not *force* you to accept this gift. You have to *choose* to reach out and receive Jesus' gift of forgiveness and new life. And you can only do this *by faith*. By faith you must *believe* that Jesus died on the cross for your sins and is your only hope to be forgiven and to be made right with God (Acts 16:31). By faith you must *turn* (repent) from your sins and put Jesus in the driver's seat of your life (Acts 2:38-39). You can't keep living for yourself and doing whatever *you* want to do. You must start living for Him and start doing what *He* wants you to do. By faith you must *confess* with your mouth to God and people that Jesus is your Lord (master) and Savior (Romans 10:9-10). And by faith you must obey Jesus' command to *be baptized* in water (Matthew 28:19).

When it comes down to it, water baptism can't save you any more than your good works can save you. But the water symbolizes the grave. As you go under the water in obedience to Jesus' command, you are making it clear that your old life is dead and buried. As you come up out of the water, you are declaring to anyone watching that God has raised you from spiritual death to live a brand new life, a life with Jesus at the helm (Romans 6:3-4).

> Trusting in Jesus Christ is your only hope to make it to Heaven.

If you have never made a clear, conscious decision to place your trust in Jesus Christ as your Savior and Lord, then I urge you to do so today. *Trusting in Jesus is your only hope to make it to heaven.* The LORD has offered you the greatest gift in the universe: the gift of forgiveness and new life. So don't be foolish. Instead of stubbornly clinging to your sin that will lead to spiritual death, accept Jesus' great gift of love and grace. It's a gift that you don't deserve but get to enjoy anyway. *Turn* from your sin and place Jesus in the driver's seat of your life. *Confess* with your mouth that Jesus is your Lord and Savior and obey Him by *being baptized* in water.

If you have truly placed your trust in Jesus Christ, congratulations! You are a follower of Christ, a Christian, and we are on this spiritual journey together. God's Holy Spirit living inside you empowers you to trust Him, love Him and obey Him every day of your life. And together we are called by Christ to share this life-saving message with others. Jesus Christ is "the way and the truth and the life." Nobody can make it to Heaven without Him. Won't you share this most important life lesson with others?

Even if you forget to share the other thirty-five, you must never forget to share this one.

ENDNOTES

1. Hamilton, Victor P. *The Book of Genesis Chapters 1-17* (The New International Commentary on the Old Testament), William B. Eerdmans Publishing Co., Grand Rapids, MI (1990), p.420.
2. Hallesby, Ole. *Prayer*, Augsburg Fortress, Minneapolis, MN (1994), pp. 18-19.